Supporting Children with Dyspraxia and Motor Co-ordination Difficulties

Completely revised and updated in light of the new 2014 SEND Code of Practice, this new edition supports teachers in making good provision for children and young people with a range of co-ordination difficulties.

Offering practical tips and strategies on how to meet the needs of children and young people with dyspraxia and other co-ordination difficulties in a range of educational settings, this book features timesaving checklists, templates and photocopiable resources to support professional development. The wide-ranging and accessible chapters explore topics including:

- Identification of different types of motor co-ordination difficulties
- Implications for classroom practice
- Understanding core skill development
- Assessment practices

Written by practitioners, for practitioners, it also contains a wealth of tried and tested strategies and provides clear best-practice guidance for developing outstanding provision in inclusive settings.

Susan Coulter – Senior Support Teacher for the Education Service for Physical Disability, Hull City Council, UK

Lesley Kynman – Senior Support Teacher for the Education Service for Physical Disability, Hull City Council, UK

Elizabeth Morling – Series Editor, SEN Consultant and former Head of the Education Service for Physical Disability, Hull City Council, UK

Rob Grayson – Team Leader for the Integrated Physical and Sensory Services, Hull City Council, UK

Jill Wing – Senior Support Teacher for the Integrated Physical and Sensory Services, Hull City Council, UK

Other titles published in association with the National Association for Special Educational Needs (nasen):

Language for Learning in the Secondary School: A practical guide for supporting students with speech, language and communication needs
Sue Hayden and Emma Jordan
2012/pb: 978-0-415-61975-2

Using Playful Practice to Communicate with Special Children
Margaret Corke
2012/pb: 978-0-415-68767-6

The Equality Act for Educational Professionals: A simple guide to disability and inclusion in schools
Geraldine Hills
2012/pb: 978-0-415-68768-3

More Trouble with Maths: A teacher's complete guide to identifying and diagnosing mathematical difficulties
Steve Chinn
2012/pb: 978-0-415-67013-5

Dyslexia and Inclusion: Classroom Approaches for Assessment, Teaching and Learning, 2ed
Gavin Reid
2012/pb: 978-0-415-60758-2

Promoting and Delivering School-to-School Support for Special Educational Needs: A practical guide for SENCOs
Rita Cheminais
2013/pb 978-0-415-63370-3

Time to Talk: Implementing outstanding practice in speech, language and communication
Jean Gross
2013/pb: 978-0-415-63334-5

Curricula for Teaching Children and Young People with Severe or Profound and Multiple Learning Difficulties: Practical strategies for educational professionals
Peter Imray and Viv Hinchcliffe
2013/pb: 978-0-415-83847-4

Successfully Managing ADHD: A handbook for SENCOs and teachers
Fintan O'Regan
2014/pb: 978-0-415-59770-8

Brilliant Ideas for Using ICT in the Inclusive Classroom, 2ed
Sally McKeown and Angela McGlashon
2015/pb: 978-1-138-80902-4

Boosting Learning in the Primary Classroom: Occupational therapy strategies that really work with pupils
Sheilagh Blyth
2015/pb: 978-1-13-882678-6

Beating Bureaucracy in Special Educational Needs, 3ed
Jean Gross
2015/pb: 978-1-138-89171-5

Transforming Reading Skills in the Secondary School: Simple strategies for improving literacy
Pat Guy
2015/pb: 978-1-138-89272-9

Supporting Children with Speech and Language Difficulties, 2ed
Cathy Allenby, Judith Fearon-Wilson, Sally Merrison and Elizabeth Morling
2015/pb: 978-1-138-85511-3

Supporting Children with Dyspraxia and Motor Co-ordination Difficulties, 2ed
Susan Coulter, Lesley Kynman, Elizabeth Morling, Rob Grayson and Jill Wing
2015/pb: 978-1-138-85507-6

Developing Memory Skills in the Primary Classroom: A complete programme for all
Gill Davies
2015/pb: 978-1-138-89262-0

Language for Learning in the Primary School: A practical guide for supporting pupils with language and communication difficulties across the curriculum, 2ed
Sue Hayden and Emma Jordan
2015/pb: 978-1-138-89862-2

Supporting Children with Autistic Spectrum Disorders, 2ed
Elizabeth Morling and Colleen O'Connell
2016/pb: 978-1-138-85514-4

Understanding and Supporting Pupils with Moderate Learning Difficulties in the Secondary School: A practical guide
Rachael Hayes and Pippa Whittaker
2016/pb: 978-1-138-01910-2

Assessing Children with Specific Learning Difficulties: A teacher's practical guide
Gavin Reid, Gad Elbeheri and John Everatt
2016/pb: 978-0-415-67027-2

Supporting Children with Down's Syndrome, 2ed
Lisa Bentley, Ruth Dance, Elizabeth Morling, Susan Miller and Susan Wong
2016/pb: 978-1-138-91485-8

Provision Mapping and the SEND Code of Practice: Making it work in primary, secondary and special schools, 2ed
Anne Massey
2016/pb: 978-1-138-90707-2

Supporting Children with Medical Conditions, 2ed
Susan Coulter, Lesley Kynman, Elizabeth Morling, Francesca Murray, Jill Wing and Rob Grayson
2016/pb: 978-1-13-891491-9

Supporting Children with Dyspraxia and Motor Co-ordination Difficulties

Second edition

Susan Coulter, Lesley Kynman, Elizabeth Morling, Rob Grayson and Jill Wing

LONDON AND NEW YORK

This edition published 2015
by Routledge
2 Park Square, Milton Park, Abingdon, Oxon OX14 4RN

and by Routledge
711 Third Avenue, New York, NY 10017

Routledge is an imprint of the Taylor & Francis Group, an informa business

First published 2005 by David Fulton Publishers

British Library Cataloguing in Publication Data
A catalogue record for this book is available from the British Library

Library of Congress Cataloging-in-Publication Data
A catalogue record for this book has been requested

ISBN: 978-1-138-85508-3 (hbk)
ISBN: 978-1-138-85507-6 (pbk)
ISBN: 978-1-315-72054-8 (ebk)

Typeset in Helvetica
by Cenveo Publisher Services

MIX
Paper from
responsible sources
FSC
www.fsc.org   FSC® C013604

Printed and bound by CPI Group (UK) Ltd, Croydon, CR0 4YY

Contents

Foreword

This book was initially written by members of the Education Service for Physical Disability, based in Hull:

- Susan Coulter
- Lesley Kynman
- Elizabeth Morling

with thanks to senior adviser John Hill for his support and encouragement throughout.

It is one of a series of titles providing an up-to-date overview of special educational needs (SEN) for special educational needs co-ordinators (SENCOs), teachers and other professionals, and parents. For details of other titles, please see page ii.

This book has now been updated to reflect new legislation and current trends in education by:

- Rob Grayson, Team Leader (Integrated Physical and Sensory Services)
- Jill Wing, Senior Support Teacher (Integrated Physical and Sensory Services)
- Elizabeth Morling, SEN consultant and series editor.

Introduction

This book is intended to support teachers in the development of children's motor co-ordination skills. The approach used recognises that the acquisition of gross motor skills underpins the development of fine motor and independence skills. The term 'co-ordination difficulty' has been used in preference to dyspraxia or developmental co-ordination disorder in recognition of the fact that many children will have difficulties which have not been diagnosed or labelled.

Research suggests that between 5 and 6 per cent of the school population will have motor co-ordination difficulties, to a greater or lesser degree, arising from dyspraxia. Add to this figure the children who have motor co-ordination difficulties associated with dyslexia, attention deficit hyperactivity disorder (ADHD), autism and difficulties resulting from medical conditions such as cerebral palsy, hyper-mobility syndromes and developmental delays, and the percentage of affected children increases.

It is not always necessary to have a diagnosis of a pupil's condition to be able to move forward. There may be differing professional opinions, or possibly overlapping conditions, which may be identified as the pupil progresses through school and difficulties become more apparent. However, the teacher's approach should always be the same: identify the problems experienced by the pupil and where possible put appropriate intervention strategies in place.

It is likely that every teacher in a primary school will be able to identify several children in his/her class who experience difficulties with motor planning and co-ordination skills.

It is anticipated that users of this book will 'dip into' sections relating to their area of concern. However, it is important to read the sections on 'Making sense of the senses' and 'Understanding physical development' to gain an awareness of the underlying processes involved.

Current teaching styles acknowledge multiple intelligences, understanding that children learn in different ways. Some are visual learners, others may be auditory learners, while many respond to kinaesthetic experiences. A multi-sensory approach is recommended wherever appropriate. Activities are suggested which can be adapted to the developmental stage of the child.

Legislation supporting the needs of these pupils

The Equality Act 2010

This act outlines 'The requirement to promote equal opportunities and to provide reasonable adjustments for those with disabilities.'

Special educational needs, as defined by the 2014 Department of Education's Special Educational Needs Code of Practice, refers to children who have a learning difficulty. This means that they either

> have a significantly greater difficulty in learning than the majority of children of the same age, or have a disability which prevents or hinders them from making use of educational facilities of a kind generally provided for children of the same age in schools within the area of the local education authority.

Teachers' Standards, Department of Education, 2012

This states that 'A teacher must ... set goals that stretch and challenge pupils of all backgrounds, abilities and dispositions'. A teacher must also 'Adapt teaching to respond to the strengths and needs of all pupils' – that is,

> know when and how to differentiate appropriately, using approaches which enable pupils to be taught effectively;
> have a clear understanding of the needs of all pupils, including those with special educational needs; .... and evaluate distinctive teaching approaches to engage and support them.

Part I

An overview of co-ordination difficulties

1 Making sense of the senses

A child with motor co-ordination difficulties presents as inattentive and clumsy, sometimes failing to make the academic progress that one suspects he/she is capable of. Parents and teachers can be puzzled as to the reasons for this behaviour. To understand the causes of this type of developmental difficulty one must look at the way in which the senses work together to influence learning.

There are three main senses which need to work effectively together to allow us to experience, interpret and respond to stimuli in our environment. This process is known as sensory integration.

1. Sense of touch (tactile)

The tactile system sends information to the brain, via cells in the skin. This information includes light touch, pain, temperature and pressure. It is this sense which enables us to rummage in a bag to find a pen or a coin without looking.

When the tactile system is not working properly, a child may hate to be cuddled, dislike getting his/her hands dirty and avoid playing with certain textures. He/she may also be sensitive to particular textures in clothing and refuse to eat certain textured foods. The child may be unable to moderate his/her own touch, resulting in rough play, sometimes misinterpreted by others as aggression.

The term 'tactile defensiveness' is used to describe a condition where a child is extremely sensitive to the lightest of touches.

When the tactile system is immature, abnormal neural signals are sent to the cortex in the brain, which can interfere with other brain processes. (The cortex is the part of the brain that interprets information.) This interference can lead to the brain being over-stimulated, which results in the person having difficulties organising, concentrating and dealing with physical contact with others.

2. Sense of movement (vestibular)

The vestibular system uses structures in the inner ear to detect movement and changes in the position of the head. It enables us to remain upright, to adjust our position, to balance and to interpret movement. The vestibular system helps to maintain muscle tone, co-ordinate the two sides of the body (bilateral co-ordination), and holds the head up against gravity. When the vestibular system is working effectively, a child can look up at the board then return to a book without losing his/her place. He/she can balance on one leg for long enough to kick a ball.

Immaturities in the vestibular system can be seen in two ways: hyper-reaction and hypo-reaction, over- and under-reaction respectively. Some children are hypersensitive to vestibular stimulation and may be frightened of ordinary movements, e.g. using slides, swings, steps and slopes. They may also be apprehensive about walking on uneven or unstable surfaces, e.g. gravel paths or sandy beaches. The child who reacts like this can appear fearful in open spaces, e.g. when in a gym or hall. The other extreme is a child who seeks intense sensory experiences by twirling, jumping and spinning in order to stimulate the vestibular system.

3. Sense of position (proprioceptive)

When a person moves, (proprioceptive) signals are sent from the muscles, tendons and joints to the brain to enable us to know what our body is doing. The proprioceptive system could be described as an internal sense of vision. It enables us to carry out actions without having to look, e.g. fastening the top button of a shirt or putting on a jumper over the head.

When the proprioceptive system is not working correctly, a child may appear clumsy, fall often, have limited understanding of his/her position in space, and bump into furniture or brush along the wall when walking in a corridor. The child may have difficulty handling small objects, leading to problems with independence skills and fine motor skills.

Another aspect of proprioception is 'praxis' or motor planning. This is the ability to plan and execute motor tasks. This is essential to learning new skills.

In summary, sensory integration takes place in the following way:

- **Input** – information from the sensory system goes into the brain via sensory pathways.
- **Processing** – the information from the senses is processed and sent to other centres within the brain where it is 'made sense of' and translated into perception and learning. This is a two-way journey, with information being sent back to the sensory systems to enable modification of movement and behaviour.
- **Output** – the brain then enables the child to carry out integrated actions, e.g. movements, interaction and functions.

When there is a problem in processing information from one of the sensory systems, the result can be poor functioning in a number of areas, as the sensory pathways are all interconnected.

References

Wright, Sally (June 1989) *Physiotherapy: Applied to the Treatment of the Child with Dyspraxia*, Dyspraxia Trust.

2 Understanding physical development

Once an understanding of how the sensory systems work together to allow the child to interact with his/her environment has been established, the stages of normal physical development need to be considered. An understanding of these stages may

Normal growth and development

1. Motor skills develop in a cephalo-caudal direction (head to toe). The baby gains head control, then shoulder control before gaining pelvis stability, walking and controlled hand skills.

2. Control or core stability is gained in a proximal-distal direction (starting with joints nearest the body – leading to those furthest away). A child learns to control the shoulders, then the elbows, followed by wrists and finally hands and fingers.

3. Fine motor control develops in a medial-distal direction (from the midline outwards).

4. A child's early movements involve the whole body; the child then learns to separate (disassociate) movements.

He/she learns to reach for an object first with the whole body:
- then with two arms;
- then with one;
- then learns to grasp an object;
- later learns to release the object.

help teachers prioritise areas of skill development. Age-referenced stages of normal development in the areas of gross motor, fine motor and independence skills precede the relevant sections.

Reference

Klein, M.D. (1982) *Pre-writing Skills: Skill Starters for Motor Development*, Communication Skill Builders.

3 Identifying children with co-ordination difficulties

The table below is intended to help teachers build up a profile of the child who is experiencing motor co-ordination difficulties. Possible difficulties have been categorised into the stage in which they are typically seen. It should be noted that children in key stages 1 and 2 are likely to experience some of the difficulties listed in the Foundation Stage section. Similarly, some pupils in key stages 3 and 4 will experience difficulties from earlier key stages. Corresponding sections of the book provide classroom strategies which can be used to target specific areas of development. Appendix 2 provides pro-formas for a pupil profile.

Area of development	Possible difficulties seen at the Foundation Stage
Sensory	• very excitable, making shrill or loud noises, hand flapping • cannot sit still during circle or story time • limited concentration, flitting from one activity to another • distressed by high levels of noise • dislikes being touched or avoids certain textures • fiddles, chews objects or clothes • poor safety awareness or a fear of heights • fussy eater.
Gross motor skills	• clumsy movements, bumps into objects, falls, trips • easily knocked off-balance • difficulty climbing on a small climbing frame • difficulty getting into or onto play equipment and chairs • jumps from inappropriate heights with no sense of danger • has to squat to pick up toys from the floor • difficulty getting up from the floor without using hands • difficulty jumping with both feet together • difficulty pedalling a tricycle • climbs the stairs leading with one foot • difficulty throwing, catching and kicking a large ball.
Fine motor skills	• uncertain of hand dominance • avoids jigsaws and construction toys • poor pencil grip • unable to use scissors • struggles to build tower of six one-inch cubes.

Area of development	Possible difficulties seen at the Foundation Stage
Independence skills	• difficulty taking off coat and hanging it on a peg • struggles with undressing • unable to use the toilet independently • messy eater, prefers to finger-feed • spills drinks.
Communication	• plays alone, rather than in a group • lack of imaginative play • difficulty following simple routines and instructions • unclear speech, cannot speak in sentences • avoidance of eye contact.

Area of development	Possible difficulties seen at Key Stages 1 and 2
Sensory	• easily distracted, lacks persistence • unable to use space effectively in PE or playground • difficulty judging distance and direction • difficulty sitting still • dislikes being touched • can be rough in play without realising • irrational fear of open space or heights • poor self-image, attention-seeking behaviour, withdrawn, underactive, reluctant to participate • lacks inhibition • poor visual tracking • difficulty copying from the board • dribbles from mouth.
Gross motor skills	• awkward, clumsy, bumps into people and objects • difficulty hopping, jumping, skipping • poor balance • poor ball skills • difficulty learning new tasks or sequences.
Fine motor skills	• poor sitting posture • uncertain of hand dominance • immature pencil grasp and poor pencil control • poor drawing skills, messy when using paints • difficulty using scissors • avoids handwriting tasks • difficulty setting out work in books • unable to construct a model following a diagram or plan.
Independence skills	• slow, messy eater • slow to change for PE, mixes up order and orientation of clothes • avoids using the toilet at school.

Area of development	Possible difficulties seen at Key Stages 1 and 2
Communication	• poor eye contact • daydreams • poor articulation, difficulties organising speech • slow to process information and give feedback (verbal or physical) • develops avoidance strategies • asks excessive questions.
Organisation	• unable to remember messages • forgets or cannot find dinner money; PE equipment • cannot cope with changes of routine • difficulty selecting equipment for a lesson or activity • poor sequencing skills.

Area of development	Possible difficulties seen at Key Stages 3 and 4
Sensory	• low self-esteem • little sense of personal safety • poor road sense as a pedestrian or cyclist • difficulty coping with board work in class.
Gross motor skills	• difficulty in PE and games activities • reluctant to participate in team games • evidence of motor stereotypes such as hand-flapping.
Fine motor skills	• difficulty keeping up with written work • books are untidy, with work being difficult to read and mark • short written responses which do not match verbal ability • unable to manipulate ruler, compass, protractor • struggles in practical subjects.
Independence skills	• avoids removing jumper/sweatshirt in very hot weather • avoids eating with cutlery • personal hygiene lacks attention.
Communication	• unable to follow complex instructions • difficulty sequencing events, particularly in written format • poor speech production • socially isolated • preoccupied with topics or subjects.
Organisation	• carries all belongings for fear of forgetting something • loses books and writing equipment • has an unkempt appearance • encroaches into his/her neighbour's personal space.

4 Overlapping conditions

Pupils with any of the conditions mentioned below will have some overlap in the difficulties experienced (listed centrally). Conditions may also co-exist. There may be between five and eight pupils in the average class with a mixture of conditions that have educational implications requiring action.

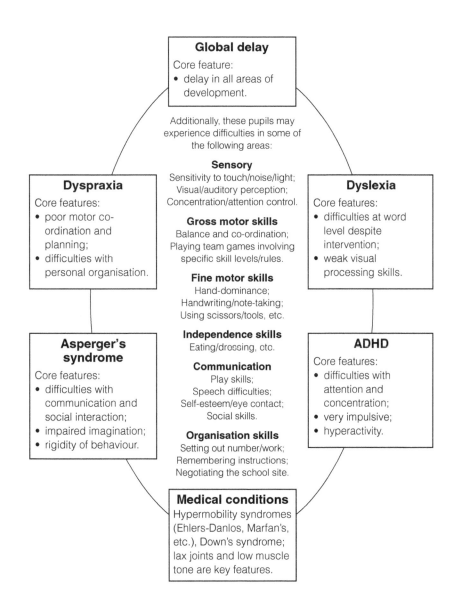

Global delay

Core feature:
- delay in all areas of development.

Additionally, these pupils may experience difficulties in some of the following areas:

Sensory
Sensitivity to touch/noise/light;
Visual/auditory perception;
Concentration/attention control.

Gross motor skills
Balance and co-ordination;
Playing team games involving specific skill levels/rules.

Fine motor skills
Hand-dominance;
Handwriting/note-taking;
Using scissors/tools, etc.

Independence skills
Eating/dressing, etc.

Communication
Play skills;
Speech difficulties;
Self-esteem/eye contact;
Social skills.

Organisation skills
Setting out number/work;
Remembering instructions;
Negotiating the school site.

Dyspraxia

Core features:
- poor motor co-ordination and planning;
- difficulties with personal organisation.

Dyslexia

Core features:
- difficulties at word level despite intervention;
- weak visual processing skills.

Asperger's syndrome

Core features:
- difficulties with communication and social interaction;
- impaired imagination;
- rigidity of behaviour.

ADHD

Core features:
- difficulties with attention and concentration;
- very impulsive;
- hyperactivity.

Medical conditions
Hypermobility syndromes (Ehlers-Danlos, Marfan's, etc.), Down's syndrome; lax joints and low muscle tone are key features.

5 Teaching pupils with co-ordination difficulties

The Teachers' Standards, Department of Education 2012, state that 'A teacher must ... set goals that stretch and challenge pupils of all backgrounds, abilities and dispositions'. A teacher must also 'Adapt teaching to respond to the strengths and needs of all pupils' – that is,

- 'know when and how to differentiate appropriately, using approaches which enable pupils to be taught effectively';
- 'have a clear understanding of the needs of all pupils, including those with special educational needs; those of high ability; those with English as an additional language; those with disabilities; and be able to use and evaluate distinctive teaching approaches to engage and support them.'

The Department of Education/Department of Health SEN Code of Practice of 2014 (CoP 2014) states that 'Teachers are responsible and accountable for the progress and development of the pupils in their class, even where pupils access support from teaching assistants or specialist staff', and determines that:

> High quality teaching, differentiated for individual pupils, is the first step in responding to pupils who have or may have SEN. Where pupils fail to make adequate progress despite high quality teaching targeted at their areas of weakness, the class teacher, working with the SENCO, should assess whether the child has a significant learning difficulty. There should then be agreement about the SEN support required for the child. Once a potential special educational need is identified, four types of action should be taken to put effective support in place – Assess, Plan, Do, Review. This is known as the graduated approach called SEN support.

This book offers strategies to support differentiation in order to address the needs of children with co-ordination difficulties within good classroom practice. The strategies will also be used when planning within the graduated approach required by the SEN Code of Practice.

Professional development

'Schools are responsible for deciding what external support to seek and for setting their own priorities for the continuous professional development of their staff.' It is likely that individual staff will identify their own professional development training needs in order to support children with co-ordination difficulties, e.g. enabling children to access the PE curriculum, assessing handwriting skills, promoting independent learning. From here the SENCO will be able to address whole-school training issues by organising INSET, which enables teachers to provide high quality teaching, differentiated for individual pupils' (SEN CoP 2014).

Schools may wish to build up a bank of resources (e.g. cue cards, visual timetables, differentiated PE activities, specialist scissors, pencil grips) which may support the differentiation process.

School approach to SEN

'All schools have a legal duty to publish information on their websites about the implementation of the governing body's or the proprietor's policy for pupils with SEN' (SEN CoP 2014).

6 Assessing, planning, teaching and reviewing

It should be noted that, on the whole, the strategies suggested in this book are derived from good classroom practice. In the Foundation Stage these activities can be incorporated into existing learning experiences, providing a suitably differentiated curriculum which will support the physical development of most children.

> Where a pupil is identified as having SEN, schools should take action to remove barriers to learning and put effective special educational provision in place. This SEN support should take the form of a four-part cycle through which earlier decisions and actions are revisited, refined and revised with a growing understanding of the pupil's needs and of what supports the pupil in making good progress and securing good outcomes. This is known as the graduated approach.
>
> (SEN CoP 2014)

Involvement of health professionals

Some children arrive to school with a specific medical diagnosis with associated co-ordination difficulties, e.g. Down's syndrome, Marfan's syndrome or autism. Evidence collected through the graduated approach to meeting SEN may, in time, indicate a need for referral to a relevant health professional such as the Occupational Therapy Service or Physiotherapy Service. Referrals are usually made by the GP at the parents' request.

7 Planning for pupils with co-ordination difficulties

Once a potential special educational need is identified, four types of action should be taken to put effective support in place – Assess, Plan, Do, Review. This is the graduated approach called SEN Support.

It is for the school or academy to determine their own approach to record keeping. But the provision made for pupils with SEN should be accurately recorded and kept up to date.

(NASEN summary of the CoP 2014)

The provision could be recorded in, for example, a Personalised Learning Plan (these plans will vary between local authorities and from school/academy to school/academy). When devising plans:

- An assessment should determine the exact needs of the pupil; observations and the use of checklists found in this book may inform this.
- The plan should include information about:
  - short-term targets set for and discussed with the pupil;
  - teaching strategies to be used;
  - provision to be put in place;
  - when the plan is to be reviewed;
  - success and/or exit criteria.
- Targets may address priorities from the following areas:
  - sensory development;
  - gross motor skills;
  - fine motor/recording skills;
  - independence skills;
  - communication skills;
  - organisational skills.
- The pupil should take part in the target setting and review process where possible.
- Parents should also be included in the target setting and review process, and encouraged to support targets at home. They should be given copies of the learning plan.
- Three or four targets should be included in the plan.
- Plans should be composed and reviewed at least twice a year.
- Pupils in Early Years settings will need targets to be reviewed at least four times a year and kept continually under review.
- Targets should be achievable, measurable and relevant to the pupil. If pupils are not achieving by the time of review, targets may be too difficult and need breaking down.
- It may be relevant to incorporate programmes into the plan from health professionals, e.g. occupational therapist, speech and language therapist, physiotherapist.

17

The following pages contain pen pictures of pupils with a range of difficulties and corresponding plans to address their needs.

Pen picture (Key Stage 1)

Hakim	Strategies to look into
Hakim is 7 years old. He has problems with attention and listening and with gross and fine motor skills.	
Hakim has had speech therapy for a number of years and in school has support to improve listening skills. He has support from a teaching assistant in the classroom, within a small group, on a daily basis.	Developing attention and listening skills (page 44)
Generally, his teacher describes his gross motor movements as being very unco-ordinated. He always has his shirt hanging out, shoes on the wrong feet and has problems putting on his coat.	Developing dressing skills (page 112)
Hakim says that he does not like sitting still. He is distractible, always moving and his attention flits from one thing to another in swift succession. When with an adult Hakim gives a constant running commentary of his observations.	Classroom organisation: sitting position and keeping hands busy (page 26)
His writing is large and poorly formed with erratic spacing and many reversals of letters. Hakim has significant difficulties copying simple shapes, in particular those involving diagonals.	Write from the Start programme on a daily basis Alternative recording strategies with use of a laptop (page 92) Improve keyboard skills through the use of the BBC Dance Mat three times a week
His drawings are idiosyncratic; people have completely irregular body shapes, with legs like ladders or a single solid oblong.	Developing body awareness (page 142)
Although Hakim has learned to run, he does so with flat feet with arms held high. He can jump but not hop. Hakim is able to catch a large ball with extended arms and throw two-handed.	Gross motor skill development programme (page 50)
Although skills are relatively poor, confidence is not affected and Hakim is very willing to persevere with activities in an effort to improve performance.	

Heathfield School

Name: **Hakim**

Nature of pupil's difficulties: Hakim has co-ordination difficulties, resulting in:

- poor letter formation, many reversals of letters, inability to produce letters with diagonals;
- poor gross motor skills, can only balance on one leg for one second;
- poor body image, inability to put shoes on correct feet.

Targets	Strategies	Resources	Evaluation
Handwriting To complete 'Write from the Start' To be able to cross the midline of his body	• Complete worksheet three times a week • In PE, play 'Hokey Cokey' and 'Pass the Hot Potato' in a ring • 'Simon Says …' actions involving opposite sides of the body	• 'Write from the Start' book 1, • 'Ultra' pencil grip • TA support	
Keyboard skills To type short phrases using a computer keyboard	• Practise typing for ten minutes a day • Use of Clicker programme to record work in topic work, e.g. history	• Dance Mat programme downloaded from the Internet • Use of Clicker 6 with grids produced which are relevant to the class topic • Access to ICT equipment	
Gross motor skills To balance on one leg for three seconds	• Small-steps programme	• TA support with a small group to develop skills	
Independence skills To put shoes on the correct feet	• Put red stickers on the instep of both shoes and instruct Hakim to 'put the stickers together' before putting shoes on	• Red stickers	

Pupil involvement: To agree to practise his typing skills at home.

Parental involvement: Parents to continue dressing objective routinely and record progress. Reward for success. Encourage typing practise.

Pen picture (Key Stage 2)

Sam	Strategies to look into
Sam is 10 years old. His gross motor milestones had been delayed; at eight months old he was not sitting and did not crawl.	
Sam likes to walk close to the wall when moving around school.	Making sense of the senses: sense of position (page 5)
He finds it hard to skip and jump and has found it very difficult to learn to swim.	Gross motor skills (page 52)
Sam's writing is a mixture of printing and joined script. He forms letters incorrectly and finds it difficult to space words. His writing deteriorates in quality if he is doing a long piece of work.	Visual perception (page 39) Alternative recording strategies (page 92)
Sam is a willing and hard-working child; however, his performance is variable. He finds maths difficult. He can rote learn, e.g. tables, but finds it difficult to solve problems and to complete tasks requiring sequencing and ordering.	Maths (page 29)
He appears to 'switch off' for short periods of time when listening to class input.	Attention and listening skills (page 44)
Sam's organisational skills are poor. He finds it difficult to remember notes/homework, etc. At present this is remedied by close co-operation between Mum and his class teacher. He finds it extremely difficult to follow class instructions and organise himself to complete a task.	Organisational skills (page 144)
Sam finds it difficult to dress himself successfully; he puts trousers on inside out and back to front, socks on with the heel at the top, shoes on the wrong feet.	Dressing skills (page 112)
Sam still finds it impossible to use a knife and fork, resorting to a spoon or fingers; he also becomes very messy in the process.	Eating skills (page 147)

Sunhill Academy

Name: Sam

Nature of pupil's difficulties: Sam has developmental co-ordination disorder, resulting in

- difficulty producing a longer piece of writing which has a pleasing appearance;
- difficulty dressing after PE;
- difficulty sequencing events for a story.

Targets	Strategies	Resources	Evaluation
To size letters correctly when writing a short piece of work	• Use of 'Write from the Start' programme on daily basis with adult oversight • Use of ICT for recording longer pieces of work • Daily practice of typing skills	• 'Write from the Start' programme • ICT equipment available • Dancemat programme	
To put jumper on with correct orientation after PE	• Teach how to take off jumper and lay it out on the desk ready to put back on • Teach how to put arms in first and pull over head	• Adult support before and after PE	
To sequence five pictures about an event	• Sequencing pictures/photographs of everyday activities, visits • Sequencing ideas for story writing in picture form prior to writing	• Digital camera, iPad, • Proforma for story layout, prepared pictures to sequence	

Parental involvement: Encourage laying out clothes at home. Recalling events after an outing.

Pen picture (Key Stage 3)

James	Strategies to look into
James is a Year 8 pupil who was diagnosed with developmental co-ordination disorder/dyspraxia.	
James is a pupil of average ability. He has always been slightly clumsy, but masked this in primary school by 'clowning around'. In secondary school, James stumbles a lot. He tends to bump into furniture in the classroom and bumps into walls unless focused on looking where he's going. James can be unsteady when bending to get his books out of his bag. He has been known to nearly miss his chair when sitting down, resulting in embarrassment when other pupils laugh. James is constantly fidgeting. This is often irritating for other pupils and distracting for teachers, which leads to James being told off.	Organising PE sessions: spatial problems (page 55) Making sense of the senses: sense of position (page 6) Attention and listening skills (page 44)
James frequently arrives at lessons with a just a pencil stub or biro refill in his pencil case; he says he has lots of equipment at home but never remembers to put it in his bag. He also carries all of his books with him all the time, explaining that this is the way he makes sure he never forgets anything.	Preparing for secondary transfer (page 122) Classroom organisation (page 26)
James's handwriting ranges from being legible on a good day to untidy and barely legible on others. Teachers' comments reveal that they expect James to be able to produce his best writing all the time. His letter formation is correct although he has difficulty writing on a line. James struggles to copy from the board, but can write to dictation, although it is usually very difficult to read his notes. James has tried word processing his work on the computer but is frustrated because his keyboard skills are poor, making him very slow. James's work is generally poorly presented with untidy corrections and inaccurate use of a ruler.	Visual perception (page 39) Developing keyboard skills (page 29)

Four men and a jolly boy came out of the black and pink house quickly
to see the bright violet sun, but the sun was behind a cloud.

Four men and a jolly boy came out of the black
and pink house quickly to see the bright
violet sun, but the sun was behind a cloud.

Word processing speed 26 letters per minute, handwriting speed 44 letters per minute (average 75).

Plumtree School

Name: James

Nature of pupil's difficulties: James has developmental co-ordination disorder. As a result he

- has difficulty copying from the board;
- is left-handed and struggles to produce consistently legible handwriting;
- fidgets constantly;
- has poor organisational skills.

Targets	Strategies	Resources	Evaluation
To minimise peer conflict caused by constant fidgeting and arm conflict	• Sit in the centre of the classroom, towards the front • Provide a piece of Blu-Tack or similar to enable 'quiet' fiddling which will not disturb others • Sit to the left of right-handers	• Seating plan • Blu-Tack	
To improve keyboard skills as an alternative recording strategy – increase speed in letters per minute to 40 Avoiding copying from the board	• Daily practice using a structured small-step programme • Speed test repeated fortnightly to plot progress • Provision of PowerPoint notes instead of copying from the board • Use of pre-drawn diagrams to minimise drawing diagrams	• Typing programme on a daily basis • Access to computer/word processor • Teachers to provide PowerPoint notes where possible	
To be equipped with the correct books and equipment for each lesson	• Organise books and equipment into subject areas • Pack school bag before bedtime • Put things back into the subject folder after use	• Homework diary • Colour-coded timetable • Clear plastic wallets for each subject with coloured spot on to link with colour coding on timetable • Duplicate writing equipment into each wallet • Record sheet	

Parental involvement: Parents will check the school bag each evening. Weekly timetable to indicated equipment required each day.

8 Home–school partnership

Parents play a major part in the support of their children; this can be enhanced by a good home-school partnership, which also includes any other professionals who may be involved, e.g. occupational therapists, physiotherapists.

Strategies to help create a good partnership:

- Parental concerns about issues should be listened to and addressed.
- In the Early Years, parents and teachers may together note a child's difficulties to create a profile of the child's strengths and weaknesses.
- Some parents may see the results of anxiety and pressure reflected in their children's behaviour at home, to which there may be simple solutions.
- It may be necessary to find joint solutions to issues such as eating packed lunches instead of school lunches, length of time on homework, difficulties in following instructions appropriately.
- Parents should be encouraged to share information and/or relevant reports from professionals about their child with school staff, where this would help to develop a complete picture of the child.
- School should also ensure that they, in turn, inform parents of visits from professionals and pass on any relevant information or reports.
- Parents should be involved in the process and be a part of supporting the target-setting process.
- It would be useful to encourage participation in activities which the child enjoys and at option times follow subjects in which they find success, in order to boost self-esteem.
- Schools can help by using a home/school diary to enable a two-way communication process for the passing on of relevant information, as the pupil may have difficulties in remembering/organising.
- Teachers and parents should be sensitive to the child by not discussing his/her difficulties in his/her hearing.
- As children make transitions between schools, discussions between parents, staff from the receiving school and the school that the child is leaving will be important. They will enable knowledge of the pupil to be passed on and strategies to be put in place, to give appropriate support in the new school.
- Endeavour to pass on positive comments to parents and avoid other children making negative comments by 'telling tales'.

NB: Parents can be given handouts (see Appendix 6) in order to help their children develop gross motor skills, and support the development of organisational skills and independent dressing skills.

9 General school issues

For any pupil with an overlapping condition in which co-ordination difficulties are a core feature there are implications for management which will need consideration and forward-planning.

On-site mobility checklist

- Are there any stairs without handrails?
- Is the pupil safe on the stairs or is adult support required to ensure safety?
- Are corridors free of clutter?
- Are there any sunken mat wells that could be a trip hazard?
- Can all pupils open doors independently? Check strength of automatic door closers and have them re-adjusted if there is a problem.
- Do fire doors open easily?
- Is there a clear path around classrooms for pupils to negotiate?
- If the pupil has a physical management programme, is there somewhere for this to be carried out?
- Can the pupil move from one class to another without getting disorientated?
- Are subject areas clearly marked? It might be helpful to colour-code different areas.

Another primary concern is attitudes to and expectations of pupils, since these inform the ethos of the school and establish a warm, caring environment in which pupils can learn and grow, regardless of the difficulties they experience.

Be aware that some pupils will try to compensate for their problems by becoming the 'class clown' or by demonstrating over-boisterous behaviour, introversion or even depression. This is particularly important in KS2 as they become more aware of their own performance compared to their peers.'

A positive attitude

It is important to always maintain a positive attitude towards pupils:

- Praise whenever possible (emphasise abilities not disabilities).
- Look for strengths or areas of interest.
- Let pupils know you are interested in their difficulties.
- Be aware that pupils may be good verbally but have poor performance skills, so accept verbal evidence of attainment and use alternative means of recording (page 92).

- Try to maintain pupils' confidence; never ridicule or compare them with others (see Promoting self-esteem, page 120).
- Be aware that pupils may not be deliberately naughty but simply not *know* how to respond appropriately in a given situation.
- Be constructively critical.
- Be aware of your own attitude to pupils' problems.

Expectations of pupils

- Have high expectations – do not put pupils into a lower ability group just because performance is poor.
- Establish baselines, e.g. check whether pupils know the alphabet, the days of the week and months of the year in correct sequence; whether they can tell the time; whether independence skills – e.g. dressing and eating – are developed (page 105).
- Some pupils have great difficulty with numbers (e.g. setting out work, learning number bonds, tables), reading music or anything involving the interpretation of symbols.
- Others may have difficulties copying/drawing diagrams and may need intervention programmes to develop visual perception/spatial awareness.
- Pupils may tire easily due to the effort of keeping up, and consequently may be inconsistent in day-to-day performance.
- Be aware of the possibility of pupils developing avoidance techniques.
- Set achievable goals and try to improve one area of work at a time.

Classroom organisation

Pupil-friendly environments help pupils feel relaxed.

- Aid organisational skills by clearly labelling drawers, etc. – colour-code if easier.
- Provide a quiet area, e.g. a book corner or library with few distractions, to reduce stimulation if necessary.
- Ensure that key words and main points are included in classroom displays for each topic/module.
- Sit pupils at the front of the class so they have a good view of the board and can focus attention on the teacher – always facing the board, not at an angle to it, since this distorts visual perception.
- Ensure pupils are in a good sitting position for working – at the right table height, sitting with straight back and feet flat (see page 72).
- If a pupil has difficulty sitting still or is constantly touching things at story time, give him/her something to play with which is fairly discreet, e.g. a piece of Blu-Tack, a stress ball.

Confidence and independent work skills

These skills and the confidence to use them can be aided by:

- splitting up work, if possible, into manageable tasks – a 'small-steps' approach makes objectives achievable and builds confidence;
- ensuring written material is visually clear and uncluttered, e.g. break up large blocks of written text into manageable pieces;

- presenting work modules in a multi-sensory format wherever possible;
- putting key words on flashcards/alphabet/number lines, etc. on pupils' desks to provide a visual prompt;
- giving new information more than once and allowing opportunities for overlearning;
- providing pictorial cue cards for different activities – if a group would benefit from a similar approach, use a whiteboard. For this activity you need:

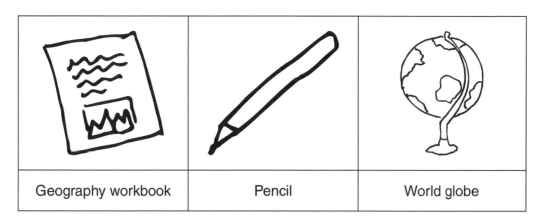

Geography workbook	Pencil	World globe

- providing older pupils with a range of *written* cue cards on a key ring for different objectives/subjects, e.g. to aid presentation:

Name (top left)   **Date (top right)**   **<u>Title centred and underlined</u>**   Draw a margin if required.   If answering numbered questions, put the number in the margin.   Leave one/two lines between the answers.

- allowing plenty of time to organise thoughts and complete the task;
- grading pupils on their own performance and progress, not in comparison with the rest of the class;
- ensuring that you have pupils' attention before giving instructions, which should be precise and concise; repeat if necessary;
- building in short breaks for physical activities/games at primary level, e.g. 'Simon Says ...', 'Activate' exercises;
- copying from the board will be problematic and should be avoided if possible, otherwise:
  - give plenty of time to copy from the board; remember that each time pupils look away from the board they may have difficulties finding their place again;
  - use different coloured pens for each line; or
  - write key words in different coloured pens.
- drawing a box when a drawing is required to help pupils organise work on a page;
- gearing questions to pupils' level so that they do not fail;
- giving individual help whenever possible;
- encouraging pupils to ask for help when stuck; teach how to do this or have a subtle way for the pupil to indicate help is required, e.g. a coloured card placed on the desk.

Problems with short-term memory

Pupils with issues in this area can be supported by:

- providing visual cues, e.g. photographs/objects of reference;
- using Post-its, e.g. to develop organisational skills;
- providing parents with vocabulary for the next teaching module, so that it can be practised prior to starting work;
- highlighting important points in notes;
- making visual timetables.

And long-term memory can be supported by:

- revisiting work done on a regular basis;
- teaching pupils how to make effective notes – concise, with numbered points and with key words underlined/highlighted;
- helping pupils to plan their revision;
- producing 'mind maps' for each module to give pupils an overview of the work covered.

Reading support

- Check that the level of reading material is appropriate; if necessary, read aloud.
- Remember that some pupils have difficulties reading small text.
- When reading long words, encourage pupils to divide syllables with a pencil line.
- Help pupils to pronounce words properly by modelling.
- Do not make the pupil read aloud in class if he/she is reluctant.
- If the pupil loses his/her place easily, use a piece of card either above or below the line being read or use a 'reading ruler'.
- Remember that a pupil may be able to read a passage correctly but not understand it.
- Do not give long lists of words to learn in spelling; two or three at a time is more appropriate.
- Some pupils benefit from a structured spelling programme which has small-step objectives and gives rewards for achievement, e.g. 'Toe by Toe', 'Starspell'.

Curricular considerations

If there are concerns about safety in the following subjects and areas, ask the SENCO to arrange a risk assessment to ensure safety guidelines are set out and adhered to – this may have staffing implications or require school management decisions. If necessary, include these guidelines in the pupil's IEP.

Specific considerations

Science/Technology/Art

- With some pupils, care will need to be taken in subjects involving the manipulation of tools and equipment to compensate for poor co-ordination, e.g.:
  - use clamps/test tube racks in science;
  - use clamps or a vice in D&T to ensure stability and best working position;
  - use a mitre saw set to stabilise wood when sawing;

- ask the school technician to make minor adaptations to tools to improve grip, e.g. extending the handle on a plane;
- use adapted equipment in food technology, e.g. vegetable workstation, multi-graters, jug blenders (page 155).

- Use bug boxes/fixed magnifiers, e.g. a 'Visualiser', which allows greater control over images and magnification.
- Provide chunky crayons/pastels/larger brushes with short handles/decorating brushes, etc., and use non-tip paint pots to support artwork.
- Provide printing stamps to make pictures if pupils lack skills and confidence to draw.
- Allow older pupils to use art/CAD programs to support design modules.
- Use Internet images to support coursework.
- Provide large bodkins and bigger mesh materials for sewing to support textiles.
- Needle threaders and embroidery hoops might also help.

Maths

- If pupils have problems developing a counting pattern, provide an abacus for them to use as a counting aid.
- Provide magnetic numbers and a board for initial work to remove the need for writing numbers.
- Allow them to work on the computer to demonstrate understanding of number operations, using e.g. '1 to 100', 'Number Shark' or 2Simple maths programs, to remove the task of writing.
- Stick a number line on pupils' desks or a 100-number square, as appropriate, to support number operations.
- Provide a series of maths templates (page 140) for younger pupils to help them establish a pattern to set out number work and place an arrow to show the direction of calculation.
- Encourage the pupil to mark off numbers (with pencil or highlighter pen) to ensure items are not counted twice.
- Provide a coloured acetate window template which can be moved around the page to assist older pupils to set out maths work.
- Provide adapted equipment, e.g. a flat compass, 'Circle Scribe', non-slip rulers (make your own by putting small pieces of sticky Dycem onto the back of a standard ruler), large-button calculators.

PE

- Have spare sandshoes, shorts, T-shirts, etc., for those pupils who always forget them.
- If slow to dress afterwards, quickly lay out clothes in the correct order and give him/her a time limit – gradually try to reduce the time by keeping a record and reward improvement.
- If the session involves team games, the teacher should select the teams rather than the pupils, who may leave those with poorer ability to last.
- In team games, place vulnerable pupils in less busy roles and gradually move them up as skills improve.
- Give spot-demonstrations of target activities and give a visual prompt to pupils with poor motor planning.

- Make allowances for pupils with delayed skills when giving instructions by including alternatives, e.g. rather than having to walk along a bench, pupils may *travel* along a bench by walking, crawling, pulling along on his/her stomach, etc.
- Have a range of differently sized/textured balls available for throwing and catching activities (see gross motor resources on page 50) and allow the pupil to choose which one to use; some balls move more slowly than others, giving pupils time to position themselves/hands correctly – note any tactile defensive response to different textures.
- Allow plenty of time for practising activities, especially if the pupil is motivated to improve skills.
- If there are problems remembering rules in team games, involve parents, so that the pupil can practise at home.

See page 54 for additional planning requirements for small-group sessions.

Homework

- Give less homework (e.g. shorter essays, or pick out the main points in note form).
- Make sure that homework instructions are understood by the pupil – it may be necessary to set up a 'buddy system' to check that homework is taken down.
- Alternatively, have homework written on slips of paper to hand out, post it on the school's website or email it to the pupil's home, whichever is the most appropriate.
- Ask parents to read the homework instructions to the pupil.
- Mark written work on content not style.
- Correct only a limited number of mistakes in written work and do not make pupils write it out again.
- Try to include positive comments about work completed.
- Use Post-its on the front of books/worksheets to remind pupils when to hand in homework at primary level; for secondary pupils (see chapter Personal organisation).

External exams

- To ensure that pupils have the opportunity to demonstrate their knowledge to the full, special arrangements may need to be requested for Year 2 and Year 6 SATs and GCSE examinations, e.g. time extension, rest breaks, use of ICT, provision of a reader/amanuensis (teach dictation skills if necessary).
- Evidence will need to be provided to demonstrate that these special arrangements have been used successfully in the classroom over a period of time.

10 Support staff: roles and responsibilities

If the pupil requires support from a classroom assistant, staff involved should:

1. Have a clear understanding of their roles and responsibilities:

- have a knowledge of their job description;
- maintain a professional demeanour with parents;
- be aware of school policies with regard to behaviour, anti-bullying, Child Protection;
- respect the confidentiality of information for all pupils.

2. Be aware of channels of communication within the school:

- ensure that information provided by parents is given to the appropriate member of staff – class teacher, SENCO;
- ensure that recommendations, communications or reports from outside agencies are passed to the teacher and SENCO;
- ensure that information given to parents is with the knowledge of the class teacher;
- ensure that there is a mechanism for disseminating information to support staff about school activities, e.g. daily diary, staffroom noticeboard.

3. Be recognised as valued members of a team:

- participate in the planning and monitoring process.

4. Be encouraged to make use of their personal skills:

- share skills, e.g. ICT, creative skills.

5. Be supported with appropriate ongoing professional development:

- observe and learn from other professionals in school and in other establishments;
- undertake training in school and through external courses.

6. Encourage the pupil's independence at all times by developing:

- work skills;
- independent self-help skills;
- personal organisation.

Teachers Standards 2012 state that teaching staff should 'Fulfil wider professional responsibilities by … deploying support staff effectively'.

The Code of Practice 2014 states: 'Where the interventions involve group or one-to-one teaching away from the main class or subject teacher, they should still retain responsibility for the pupil, working closely with any teaching assistants or specialist staff involved, to plan and assess the impact of interventions.'

11 Support staff: guidelines for working with pupils

Avoid	Instead
Sitting next to the pupil at all times.	Work with other pupils, while keeping an eye on the pupil you are assigned to.
Offering too close an oversight during breaks and lunchtimes.	Encourage interaction with peers, or allow the pupil to be solitary, follow his/her own interests and relax.
Collecting equipment for the pupil or putting it away.	Encourage the pupil to carry this out independently, e.g. ensuring drawers are clearly labelled.
Completing a task for a pupil.	Ensure work is at an appropriate level and is carried out with minimal support (note any support given).
Using language inappropriate to the pupil.	Give short instructions at the pupil's level of development, with visual prompts.
Making unnecessary allowances for the pupil.	Establish what is required using appropriate strategies and have expectations that a task will be completed.
Working in cluttered areas.	Provide a clear, predictable learning environment.
Tolerating undesirable behaviour.	Observe the pupil; determine reasons for behaviour and consider if changes can be made.
Making unrealistic demands on the pupil.	Ensure instructions are at the appropriate level and that goals are achievable.
Making decisions for the pupil.	Give the pupil opportunities to develop choice-making skills by providing structure and restricted choices.
Letting the pupil become dependent on his/her support assistant.	Encourage independent behaviour and work.

Part II

Understanding core skill development

- Sensory issues
- Gross motor skills
- Fine motor skills

12 Sensory issues

Please read 'Making sense of the senses' first.

In the classroom pupils may exhibit problems in the following areas:

- Over-/under sensitivity to touch/light/sound, e.g.:
  - disliking loud noises, seeking rough play, reacting inappropriately to another pupil coming too close.
- Visual problems including visual tracking, depth perception, visual perception (particularly important for reading and writing), problems judging distances/poor catching skills/not recognising a familiar object from a different perspective (form constancy).
- Difficulty maintaining eye contact.
- Problems with auditory perception, e.g.:
  - not hearing a car approaching/not hearing certain sounds within words or missing whole words.
- Poor attention control, e.g.:
  - not paying attention when instructions are being given, not staying on-task.

Any difficulty, once identified, needs to have strategies put in place to reduce the impact of the problem on learning.

This section covers:

- Strategies to support pupils with over-/undersensitivity to touch, light and sound
- Strategies to support pupils who have difficulties with visual perception
- Possible auditory difficulties and strategies to support development.

13 Supporting pupils with over-/under-sensitivity to touch, light and sound

Pupils may have:

oversensitivity to noise/light/touch; the pupil:	undersensitivity to noise/light/touch; the pupil:
<ul><li>does not like different textures, e.g. when eating, touching</li><li>does not like to get his/her hands sticky</li><li>is intolerant of loud noises, e.g. clapping in assemblies</li><li>avoids touching objects/peers</li><li>avoids rough-and-tumble play.</li></ul>	<ul><li>is always touching things</li><li>seeks vestibular stimulation, e.g. spinning, roundabouts, flings him/herself around</li><li>likes and seeks noise/stimulus, etc.</li><li>generally crashes around bumping into objects and people</li><li>really enjoys rough play.</li></ul>
Strategies to support the pupil:<ul><li>Sit the pupil in a quiet area with minimal visual stimulus.</li><li>Discuss different aspects of touch, e.g. things that are dry/sticky/rough/smooth; introduce new textures slowly.</li><li>Ditto with taste; encourage tasting new flavours.</li><li>Try to develop touch by having different textured resources, e.g. a variety of balls/beanbags in PE, feely bags.</li><li>Give him/her activities using clay or plasticine which require more strenuous pressure.</li><li>Allow the pupil to sit near the door in assemblies or wear ear plugs.</li><li>Structure playtimes and encourage the pupil to take part in different activities.</li></ul>	**Strategies to support the pupil:**<ul><li>Sit the pupil in the least busy part of the classroom to reduce stimulus.</li><li>Give the pupil something to play with, e.g. Blu-tack to keep hands busy.</li><li>Have a quiet area with no visual stimulus for time out/story.</li><li>Have quiet music playing in the background to promote a calm environment.</li><li>Begin morning and afternoon sessions with 2–3 minutes of stillness, e.g. breathing in and out to a count of 5 or 6, visualisation, etc.</li><li>Discuss 'personal space' and include in role play.</li><li>Pretend to be a mouse/elephant: 'How would you stroke these?', etc.</li><li>Structure playtimes to limit the opportunities for rough play by demonstrating appropriate play and the use of play equipment.</li></ul>

If the pupil does not improve, seek further advice from either a paediatric occupational therapist or the school's educational psychologist.

14 Visual perception difficulties and strategies to support development

Some pupils with co-ordination difficulties may experience problems with visual perception

Problem with:	Examples:	Strategies to support development:
Visual tracking	• tracking a ball through the air.	• use balloons/soft balls/bean bags, etc. (less threatening).
	• eyes jumping over letters/ words/lines when reading, writing or copying work.	• tracking exercises, e.g. following a torch beam, joining dots, from left to right, on a large piece of paper/whiteboard • use a 'Reading Helper' (see Appendix 9) • trial a variety of coloured acetate over-lays for reading.
	• setting out maths work (reversing/ transposing symbols).	• avoid copying from the board • provide maths templates (page 144) • multi/sensory approach to number writing • use of computer programs. NB: Pupils may need to be referred to an optician.
Visual spatial relationships	• bumping into objects/ furniture.	• create obstacle courses • provide brightly coloured furniture.
	• judging distances.	• draw a metre grid on the hall floor – place a beanbag in one square and ask the pupil to judge how far away it is • ask the pupil how far he/she needs to move to reach the beanbag.
	• finding the way around school.	• use a buddy.
	• judging positioning of objects.	• provide large-sized toys/pencils/ paint-brushes to start with • encourage the pupil to hold objects in the midline with both hands.

Problem with:	Examples:	Strategies to support development:
Figure/ground discrimination	• finding a toy/ object on a patterned carpet.	• use brightly coloured toys • ensure that there is a plain carpet in play areas.
	• finding his/her work drawer/ coat peg/books, etc.	• clearly label drawers/coat pegs with a picture and name label.
	• identifying a ball thrown to him/ her.	• use large, brightly coloured balloons/ balls, etc. • give the instruction, 'Watch for the red/ blue balloon/ball and get ready to catch it …'.
	• identifying a car approaching on the road.	• incorporate into road safety work.
	• locating furni-ture in a busy classroom.	• simplify the classroom layout leaving space around furniture for movement • use brightly coloured furniture • mark the edges of table with brightly coloured tape.
	• making sense of pictures.	• use inset boards, mosaics, jigsaws • recognise an object while slowly revealing it.
	• understanding picture sequences to make a story.	• use simple black and white line drawings • talk about what is in the picture with the pupil • ask the pupil to colour in the main object/person in the picture.
	• finding charts/ maps difficult to read.	• produce large, simple, uncluttered charts • enlarge maps and colour-code • provide a perspex grid to put over maps to help the pupil orientate him-/herself.
	• finding that words merge together on the page.	• use a ruler or 'Reading Helper' to isolate the line; point to, or use two L-shaped pieces of card to isolate words • trial different coloured acetates – one colour may make reading easier • request that the pupil be tested for scotopic sensitivity.

Problem with:	Examples:	Strategies to support development:
Form/size constancy	• recognising that an object seen close up is the same when seen in the distance or from another angle.	• match differently sized pairs (objects/ pictures) • give the pupil 3 different objects and ask him/her to match them to objects 3 metres away; increase distance and similarity/number of objects gradually • ask the pupil to match a picture on the desk to one stuck on the wall • match pictures of objects taken from different perspectives.
	• recognising that a word is the same regardless of size or font.	• provide sets of words in different fonts/ sizes/colour, etc., and ask them to match a given word • set up word searches for finding a word in different fonts • cut out the word shape and ask them to match it to the correct word.
Maintaining eye contact (some pupils find maintaining eye contact threatening, in which case in should not be insisted on)	• making either too long or too short eye contact (resulting in problems with social interaction).	• request pupils to 'Look at me' when giving instructions to the class • use puppets to encourage eye contact (less threatening) • discuss eye contact and its part in social interaction, e.g. paying attention, showing consideration, smiling, making friends • use social group work to develop social interaction skills.
Visual closure	• deducing information from incomplete visual diagrams/ pictures.	• identify a shape from part of the shape • slowly reveal pictures • complete a partially drawn shape/object.

Additionally, for writing, spatial concepts are involved:

Spatial awareness/ orientation Check: does the pupil understand positional words, e.g. beside/next to, right/left, top to bottom?	• placing writing/ drawing correctly on a page.	• draw boxes in the book/ worksheet to indicate where a drawing should go • give well-spaced, bold lines to write on rather than a blank page • put a green dot at the start of a line to indicate where writing should start and a red one for where it should finish;
	• spacing between words missing.	• check pupil knows where spaces should be • use finger/card spacer, 'spaceman' lollipop stick with spaceman head drawn on • when checking work, ask pupil to use a highlighter to show where gaps should be • use 'Write from the Start' to develop visuo-spatial skills.
	• letters reversed or upside down, mirror writing, etc.	• check for cross-laterality (eye-hand dominance – page 85), which may cause problems with left/right orientation, reversals, etc. • use a multi-sensory approach to letter writing; touch and sight using three-dimensional letters, drawing letters in the air or with the finger on the table, tracing letters' shapes in sand • give visual perception exercises, e.g. circle all the letter 'b's • have one pupil write a letter on the back of another, who should guess what it is • use 'word play' prompts, e.g. bat and ball for the letter 'b'.
Spatial relationships (understanding how two or more objects relate to one another)	• spelling and reading problems – also linked to visual memory and visual sequential memory.	• use spelling games • look at patterns in words • use simple mnemonics to aid spelling, e.g. bat and ball for 'b'.

Additional classroom strategies to support visual perception

For those pupils who have problems with visual perception there are a variety of ways in which the teacher can support them in the classroom:

- Reduce visual clutter in displays to avoid visual overload.
- Ensure that information progresses from left to right.
- Provide simple, clear worksheets and activity cards.
- Enlarge text and use double spacing.
- Seating position in the class is important. The pupil should sit facing the whiteboard and teacher, not at an angle to it, since this distorts visual perception.
- Provide a fixed-angle board for copying work (see Sitting position for classroom activities) since this reduces the range of eye movement required between model and reproduction.
- Allow the pupil to write on alternate lines, to reduce visual clutter.
- Encourage the pupil to hold the reading book upright when reading as this reduces visual distortion of text.
- Use a multi-sensory approach to pre-writing skills (see Fine motor skills) to teach individual letter shapes and spellings.
- Teaching cursive script rather than print means that the hand learns the 'shape' of the whole word, which helps with spelling. NB: Refer to the school's policy on handwriting for guidance regarding this.

15 Auditory difficulties and strategies to support development

Problem with:	Examples:	Strategies to support development:
Auditory discrimination	• recognising everyday sounds.	• match picture to sound on tape • 'Simon Says …'/'I Spy …', etc. • Chinese whispers.
	• identifying the same letter sound when at the beginning/ middle/end of a word.	• sound matching – say a sound and ask the pupil to put up his/her hand when he/she hears the sound again • 'I Spy' with initial/end letter sounds.
Rhythm	• recognising and copying.	• join in nursery rhymes/songs • play marching songs in different tempos in PE • copy a tapped pattern • tap out the syllables in names/ words, etc., on a drum.
Auditory selection (pupils may switch off and appear to daydream if there is a problem in this area)	• being able to pick out sounds/instructions, etc., from a busy background.	• use a small bell to signal that pupils listen for a new instruction.
	• picking out the sound of a car from street sounds.	• ask the pupil to clap when he/she hears a certain voice on a tape.
Auditory memory	• remembering instructions.	• Chinese whispers • shopping games – 'I Went to the Shops and I Bought an Apple …', each pupil adding something • each child adds a word to a sentence, etc.

Problem with:	Examples:	Strategies to support development:
Control of pitch	• being able to moderate voice appropriately, i.e. speak softly/loudly.	• whispering games • 'How do you speak to the person next to you/across the classroom?', etc. • act out stories with contrasting characters, e.g. Jack and the Beanstalk, Goldilocks • use puppets if pupils lack confidence.

16 Gross motor skills

Motor control is gained from the head downwards to the feet and from the midline of the body out to the fingers.

Additionally, the left side of the brain controls the right side of the body and vice versa. This effectively results in an invisible midline running down the length of the body and young children must learn to work *around* this midline. The pupil must also learn to co-ordinate both sides of the body if he/she is to walk, run or kick a ball while balancing on the other leg, etc.

This section contains:

- An overview of gross motor skills progression.
- A gross motor skill checklist to help determine the level of development of the pupil, with activities which will improve skills.

Staff will be able to judge approximate skill level through observation of the pupil in playground activities and PE sessions. Discussion with parents will also provide relevant information, e.g. delayed physical milestones, crawling stage missed out, etc. The latter has implications for bilateral co-ordination and both body and spatial awareness.

The activities described in 'Gross motor skill checklist and activities' may be included in play sessions. Try to put them into a game context where possible, e.g. 'long sitting' (sitting on the floor with back against the wall and legs out straight) to develop sitting balance while playing the 'Pass the Hot Potato' game. They could also be included in PE; pupils with physical difficulties will require extra support and encouragement to ensure the work is effective. The activities are also appropriate for small-group work.

Subsequent pages provide:

- points to bear in mind when setting up a small-group activity session for pupils with co-ordination difficulties;
- guidance for extending skills in the Early Years;
- ideas for promoting physical skills with secondary-aged pupils.

17 Overview of gross motor skills progression

Staff need to be aware of the developmental sequence for the acquisition of gross motor skills and that they are built up hierarchically, i.e.:

➜ core stability (head control, sitting balance, shoulder and hip fixation) underpins standing balance; leading to
➜ bilateral integration (walking, balancing on one leg, hopping, running, jumping, climbing, skipping, etc.);
➜ eye-hand-foot co-ordination for throwing, catching, kicking, etc.

3 months	• sits with back straight apart from lower lumber region when supported • on tummy, lifts head and upper chest using forearms to support • on back, kicks legs alternately.
6 months	• lying on back, raises head • sits with support • if hands are held, braces shoulders and pulls to sitting • on tummy, lifts head and upper body on flat hands and straight arms • when held, takes weight on feet and bounces up and down.
9 months	• sits on floor unaided for 10–15 minutes • leans forward, turns to look sideways, stretches out to pick up a toy • progresses along the floor by rolling • pulls to standing holding onto furniture • attempts to crawl • held upright, steps with alternate feet.
12 months	• sits on floor for indefinite time • can rise to sitting from lying down • pulls to standing and sits down again holding onto furniture • walks around furniture side-stepping • may stand alone • walks forward with hand held.

15 months	• kneels unaided or with minimum support on floor • can get to feet and down again without holding on • creeps upstairs safely • walks alone with uneven steps, arms held fixed or out to aid balance.
18 months	• kneels upright on flat surface without support • flexes knees and hips to pick up toy from the floor, using hands to help, then rises to feet alone • walks independently, stopping and starting safely • runs carefully in straight line, looking at ground, head in the midline.
2 years	• squats safely to play • sits on small tricycle and propels with feet on the floor • can stop/start/turn around safely • climbs on furniture and can get down safely • walks up and sometimes down stairs holding rail safely • walks into a large ball to try to kick it • throws a small ball overhand.
2½ years	• jumps with both feet together from a low step • can stand on tiptoe when shown • walks up stairs confidently holding rail • walks down stairs two feet to a step • runs, and climbs on nursery equipment safely • throws ball at body level • kicks a large ball gently.
3 years	• sits with feet crossed at ankles • stands on tiptoe • stands on preferred foot briefly • jumps when shown from bottom step of stairs safely • walks forwards/backwards/sideways with confidence • rides a tricycle using pedals • runs around obstacles safely • throws a ball overhand • catches large ball on, or between, extended arms • kicks a large ball forcibly.

4 years	• picks up objects from the floor by bending from the waist with knees extended • sits with knees crossed • stands on preferred foot for 3–5 seconds • hops on preferred foot • walks up and down stairs one foot to a step • walks and runs on tiptoe • climbs ladders/trees • increasingly skilful at throwing/catching/bouncing/kicking balls.
5 years	• stands on either foot for 8–10 seconds on preferred foot with arms folded • walks along a narrow line • skips on alternate feet • hops 2–3 metres on either foot • skilful at climbing/sliding/swinging, etc.

It is important to remember that:

• a child cannot perform a skill out of sequence;
• problems frequently arise from low muscle tone, which results in slower progress of the acquisition of skills.

Reference

Overview of gross motor skills adapted from Sheridan, M. (2005) *From Birth to Five Years*, Routledge.

18 Gross motor skills checklist and activities

Skill area to be checked:	If not, try the following activities:
Rolling – can the pupil: ☐ travel along a mat by rolling?	– roll on stomach/back on request – roll downhill on a wedge shape – play 'There Were Ten in a Bed …'
Sitting balance – can the pupil: ☐ sit on a chair maintaining a good upright position for working?	– long sitting: legs outstretched – sitting cross-legged on the floor, play 'I'm a Little Teapot' – free-sit on the floor with arms out straight at the side, rock from side to side (aeroplanes, turn right/left, etc.) – sit and balance on a wobble board.
Crawling – can the pupil: ☐ crawl forwards/backwards/ over/under/around, etc.?	– move forwards/backwards using arms only, lying on a scooter board – in the crawl position, raise left/right arm alternately – in the crawl position, raise left/right leg alternately – Superman/woman, raising opposite arm and leg – 'Cats and Camels', i.e. hump and hollow back in the crawl position – crawl over obstacles of varying heights and textures – crawl around a circuit, e.g. shipwreck (dry land and water).
☐ crawl through a tunnel?	– crawl through a hoop/line of hoops – crawl through a small tunnel made of PE equipment – crawl through partially extended tunnel.
☐ crawl along a bench?	– crawl along a line – crawl along/around the edge of a PE mat – crawl over a line of thick cushions.

Skill area to be checked:	If not, try the following activities:
Kneeling – can the pupil: ☐ maintain a kneeling position for 5 minutes?	– let the pupil high kneel with arms on the table – work at the table in a high kneeling position – from a crawl position, sit back on his/her heels.
☐ walk in a high kneeling position?	– paint at an easel in a high kneeling position – kneel on one leg and raise the other leg at right angles, hold arms out at the side – same position, fold arms and balance – work at the table in a high kneeling position – move around the table, to next activity, in high kneeling position.
Balance in walking – can the pupil: ☐ 'stop' on request when walking, e.g. 'Statues'?	– play 'Statues', traffic light game, 'What Time Is It, Mr Wolf?', etc.
☐ walk along a straight line marked on the floor?	– walk between tramlines on the floor, gradually reducing distance between lines – walk along a wide ribbon.
☐ walk on tiptoes, heels, etc.?	– rock forwards on toes – swing arms and reach as high as you can – reach high and lean forwards, staying on toes – sit on chair and raise toes; try to rise in this position – lean against the wall and raise toes.
☐ step over an obstacle?	– step over a beanbag on the floor – step over a rope on the floor, gradually raise it higher off the floor.
☐ walk along a low bench?	– walk between tramlines on a PE mat – walk over a line of cushions on the floor.
☐ walk in and out of objects?	– walk around one object and back (relay races) – walk between two obstacles – increase number of obstacles and weave between them (relay races).
☐ follow cut out footprints on the floor?	– step over ropes evenly spaced – walk one foot to a square grid, gradually reduce in size.
☐ balance a beanbag on the back of one hand?	– walk with large ball held in both hands – walk with beanbag held in both hands – walk with beanbag resting on upturned hand.
☐ balance a beanbag on his/her head?	– walk with large hat on his/her head, then smaller hat – walk with a quoit on his/her head.

Skill area to be checked:	If not, try the following activities:
Balancing on one leg – can the pupil: ☐ march, raising knees as high as possible?	– walk on the spot, gradually raising knees higher – doing this to music will help establish a rhythm, begin with fast music then slow down rhythm.
☐ walk sideways?	– single sideways step, both ways, increase number of steps (e.g. a simple line-dancing routine).
☐ follow well-spaced 'stepping stones' making giant steps, walking slowly?	– step over a series of beanbags in a line – stride from one mat to another across a gap, increase gap – walk, placing one foot in each hoop set in a line, increase gap.
Climbing – can the pupil: ☐ climb up wall bars? (Be aware that some children may have problems with depth perception as well as poor co-ordination skills.)	– climb in and out of a box – crawl through a tunnel – step over/on/off graded obstacles, steps, etc. – climb stairs one at a time.
Running – can the pupil: ☐ run safely on tiptoes?	– walk heel to toe along a line – stand on tiptoe and turn around – walk on tiptoe, increase speed.
☐ run around obstacles changing direction easily?	– walk, weaving in and out of a cone slalom course – move alternate cones out to each side, making direction changes more acute – obstacle team races, walk slowly first, then faster.
Jumping – can the pupil: ☐ jump off the bottom step holding hands?	– bend knees and reach up high quickly – run and jump over beanbag, etc.
☐ jump on the spot?	– infant trampoline – step on and off a kerb in the playground – play 'Jack in a Box'.
Throwing – can the pupil: ☐ throw a large ball at a target? (NB: use a range of balls with different textures and sizes.)	– roll a ball to partner using both hands – roll a ball around his/her feet and back – push a ball at a large target on the wall – sit on a bench and push a large ball off his/her knees towards the wall target – stand and drop the ball into a hoop, gradually increasing the distance.
☐ throw a ball underarm with preferred hand to a partner?	– throw a beanbag into a hoop, increasing the distance – throw a beanbag at a target on the wall – try using different types of ball to hit the target.

Skill area to be checked:	If not, try the following activities:
☐ throw a ball overarm with preferred hand?	– throw a beanbag as hard as possible at the floor – throw a beanbag into a large container on the floor – throw a beanbag at a target on the wall, starting close to and increasing distance.
Catching – can the pupil: ☐ catch a large ball?	– play 'Pass the Ball' over his/her head with both hands to a partner – roll a ball around his/her body – roll and stop a ball in a group circle – roll a ball along a table top and stop it at the other end – throw up and catch a balloon or a large soft ball (these move more slowly) – drop a large ball with two hands and catch, increase force used – bounce a large ball to a partner for him/her to return.
Kicking – can the pupil: ☐ kick a large ball while standing?	– kick a ball when seated on a high chair – hold on between two chairs and kick a large ball – hold one chair (same side as dominant foot) and kick the ball.
☐ run at a ball and kick it?	– walk into a balloon/large soft ball and kick it without intent – run at a balloon/large soft ball and kick it.
☐ dribble a ball?	– walk and gently kick a balloon/large soft ball, follow it and kick again – walk and dribble a balloon/large soft ball around a short slalom course.
Hopping and skipping – can the pupil: ☐ hop forwards 3 metres?	– hold the pupil's hands and ask him/her to jump, encourage him/her to try to use one leg only – hop holding onto a chair back – hop around a table holding on.
☐ skip in a straight line?	– hop on the spot and change feet after two hops – hop and change feet after one hop – hop to a rhythm around the room.

Skill area to be checked:	If not, try the following activities:
Midline awareness and bilateral integration – can the pupil:	(to ensure ability to co-ordinate both limbs by crossing the midline of the body)
☐ cross the midline of the body?	– cross-crawling – touch right elbow to left knee, etc., standing up (Brain Gym activities, etc.) – do the 'Hokey Cokey' – raise foot backwards and touch foot with the opposite hand behind his/her back – PE activities such as ribbon work, team games (e.g. pass the beanbag standing sideways) – copying actions, 'Simon Says …', etc.

Developing gross motor skills

Some pupils benefit from a more structured approach to addressing their physical difficulties, especially if confidence is low and they are reluctant to participate in group activities.

When planning a programme for small-group work, either select one activity from each skill area and vary the programme as skills progress or concentrate on one area as a 'theme'. Sensitive organisation is required to take into consideration any lack of confidence or low self-esteem.

As skills develop, transfer from small-group work to group work within a PE lesson.

Example of group session – with a focus on running balance

1. Warm-up exercises:
   a. shaking hands, arms, one leg and then the other, whole body;
   b. swing arms to cross in front of the body and then swing them up high (windmills);
   c. stretching up tall onto toes, stretching arms and legs as wide as possible.
2. Walking race in which each pupil must walk heel to toe along a line.
3. Ditto walking on hands and toes.
4. Run around the room on tiptoes.
5. Running race, there and back, around a cone at the far side of the hall.
6. Running around a slalom course of cones in relays or teams; increase the number of cones as ability improves.
7. Wind down activity, e.g.:
   a. shake arms while jogging on the spot;
   b. reach up high and stretch up tall on tiptoes, slowly bring arms down;
   c. lie down and breathe quietly for 1 minute.

- Pupils often have spatial problems, so limit the amount of equipment per session.
- Encourage pupils to work within a defined space, e.g. chalk a grid, or place a PE mat, on the hall floor and instruct them to work within the square. A chalk grid could be numbered so the pupil knows which the 'home' square is and then move as directed by the teacher.
- Always have a warm-up period, revisit previous skills learned, introduce new skills and finish with a quiet reflective wind-down prior to going back to class.
- Teach new skills in small stages if necessary; this will help to build up control.
- To demonstrate improvement to the pupil, keep a record of progress. NB: The pupil is always competing with him-/herself, not with others.

Early Years/Key Stage 1 pupils:

- If the pupil has difficulty riding a tricycle, work on these checklist activities:
  - balancing on one leg/hopping to build up upper trunk balance;
  - climbing, to build up leg muscle strength.
- Pupils with poor balance will be afraid to go on the climbing frame. Grade climbing activities, e.g. have boxes of different sizes to climb in and out of; instruct pupils to climb *around* the frame rather than *up*.
- To develop spatial awareness further, get the pupils to work within a hoop, e.g. be a statue, march/run/jump/hop on the spot, climb through, walk around the outside clockwise/anticlockwise, etc.
- With a pupil showing overflow of movement to upper limbs, e.g. arms moving like windmills when running, instruct them to keep their elbows bent and tucked in to their sides.
- For those whose arms flap when asked to balance on one leg, instruct them to keep arms straight down by the sides of the body, like a soldier.
- If this does not work, give the pupil water-filled milk cartons to carry to weigh down his/her arms; gradually reduce the amount of water.
- Always involve parents so they can follow the same method. A united approach reduces confusion and helps the pupils to learn a skill more quickly.
- Encourage parents to take younger pupils to soft play areas, the adventure playground in the park, etc., and all-age pupils to swim, play football with Mum/Dad or siblings (see Appendix 6.1).

Primary/Secondary-aged pupils

- Watch for any strengths in PE and encourage the pupil to stretch him-/herself in that particular area.
- Encourage the pupil to work on developing muscle strength, e.g. weight training if the school has a multi-gym. NB: If the pupil is under the supervision of a paediatric physiotherapist or occupational therapist, discuss with them what would be most appropriate before beginning any programme.
- If no multi-gym is available, devise a fitness programme, e.g.:
  - upper body weight-bearing activities, e.g. press ups;
  - endurance activities, e.g. running, football activities. These improve both motor skills and all-round self-confidence.

- Always try to work with a small group rather than individuals since this reassures the pupil that 'others have problems too'. Sessions should be based around individual needs but should lead into additional practise for skills being covered in PE lessons.
- Aim for a minimum of three short sessions a week rather than a single longer session.
- Encourage out-of-school activities which help to develop hand-eye co-ordination and confidence, e.g. golf, judo. Games on the Wii may also improve co-ordination.

19   Fine motor skills

In this section, Chapter 20 provides an overview of fine motor skill progression. Approximate ages are given as a guide to 'normal' stages of development.

There are five areas of skill development referred to in this section:

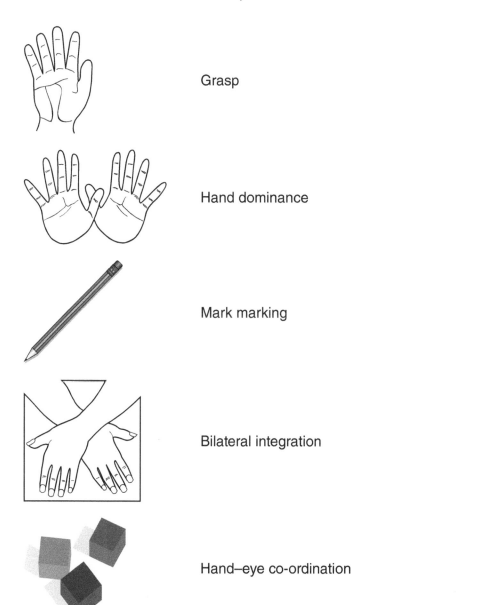

Grasp

Hand dominance

Mark marking

Bilateral integration

Hand–eye co-ordination

- Skills are organised into a hierarchical order and a key is used for clarification.
- A checklist with suggested activities to develop each skill area is included in Chapter 21.

The checklist can be used to record achievement and may also be used to identify weaknesses in a specific area of skill development. The skill focus and examples of activities to address weaknesses are again arranged in a hierarchical order.

- In many cases these activities will already be part of good classroom practice.
- There is inevitably some repetition in the suggested activities as many activities will address more than one skill area.
- Children who present difficulties within this area may have an uneven profile with gaps in skill development.
- When working with older pupils, careful planning will be required to ensure that activities are modified to provide age-appropriate interventions.

20 Overview of fine motor skills progression

6 months	holds toys in a palmar grasp (whole hand) and passes from hand to hand
	picks up objects by scooping with both hands.
9 months	isolates index finger to poke at a small object
	begins to use pincer grasp (index finger and thumb).
12 months	picks up small objects using fine pincer grasp between tip of index finger and thumb
	begins to show hand dominance.
15 months	uses pincer grasp with both hands at the same time
	scribbles backwards and forwards using a palmar grasp in either hand
	&
	builds a tower with 2 cubes following a demonstration.
18 months	shows signs of developing a crude thumb and 2-finger grasp
	picks up small objects accurately
	turns pages several at a time
	points with precision at pictures in a book
	most children will now have a hand dominance
	scribbles and makes dots
	&
	builds a tower of 3 cubes following demonstration (sometimes spontaneously).

2 years		good manipulative skills, now picks up and places objects neatly and with accuracy
		turns single pages in a book
		holds a pencil using thumb and first 2 fingers
		draws spontaneous circular scribble and dots
		imitates vertical lines and sometimes V-shapes
		builds a tower with 6 or 7 cubes.
2½ years		holds a pencil in an improved tripod grasp
		has a dominant hand
		imitates a horizontal line, a circle
		imitates 'T' and 'V'
		builds a tower of 7+ bricks using dominant hand.
3 years		picks up very small objects using pincer grasp
		can close fist and wiggle thumbs of both hands in imitation
		can hold pencil in dominant hand with 2 fingers and thumb
		draws horizontal and vertical lines
		copies 'O V H T'
		imitates 'X'
		draws a person with a head and 2 more parts or features
		builds a bridge using 3 bricks after a demonstration.
4 years		copies 'X'
		draws 'O V H T'
		draws a person with head, trunk, legs, and usually arms and fingers
		draws a recognisable house
		&
		threads small beads
		builds towers of 10+ cubes
		builds bridges spontaneously using 3 bricks.

5 years	counts fingers of one hand using index finger of other
	copies squares
	copies triangles (by 5½)
	writes a few letters spontaneously
	copies 'V T H O X L A C U Y'
	draws a person with head, trunk, legs, arms, fingers and features;
	draws a house with windows, doors, roof and chimney
	draws pictures with several items and shows an indication of background
	colours pictures staying mainly within the lines
	&
	threads a large needle
	builds 3 steps using 6 cubes following a demonstration.

Reference

Overview of fine motor skills adapted from Sheridan, M. (2005) *From Birth to Five Years*, Routledge.

21 Fine motor skills checklist and activities

Skill area to be checked:	If not, try the following activities:
Grasp – can the pupil: ☐ hold objects in a palmar grasp? (whole hand) 	– provide a wide range of toys to stimulate interest; encourage the child to reach out and grasp with both hands – pick up and release a foam ball – pick up and pass small ball from hand to hand.
☐ use index finger in isolation? (pointing)	– teach finger rhymes such as 'Two Little Dickie Birds' – use finger puppets on the index finger – press keys of a toy telephone, till, toy musical instruments – encourage finger painting – encourage recorder playing/piano/keyboard playing – teach keyboard/typing skills.
☐ hold objects in pincer grasp? (index finger and thumb)	– pop bubble wrap between finger and thumb – peg out washing (or paintings) to dry – inset jigsaws (reducing in size) – bulldog clips to fasten paper – sorting activities using small objects.
☐ hold a pencil in tripod grasp?	– use activities above to develop a tripod grip – try a range of pencil grips.
Other considerations ☐ use finger and thumb in opposition?	– touch each finger in turn using the thumb – pick up small toys using tweezers or tongs – roll plasticine or playdough between finger and thumb – play with 'popper-beads' – play with wind-up clockwork toys – fasten press-studs on clothing.

62

Skill area to be checked:	If not, try the following activities:
☐ demonstrate acceptable finger/hand strength?	– squeeze playdough, stress balls – playdough and plasticine activities – tug of war – water race where water is transferred from one container to another by filling and squeezing sponges – hand jives/hand warm-up exercises – squeezing citrus fruits on a traditional lemon squeezer – chair press-ups – write/draw with carbon paper under to encourage pressure – offer squiggle pens and light pens, which give sensory feedback with sufficient pressure – use of a paper punch and stapler.
☐ rotate wrists/forearm?	– nut and bolt toys – wring out cloths and dolls' clothes – look through a kaleidoscope – sharpen pencils.
Hand dominance – can the pupil: ☐ demonstrate hand dominance? 	– encourage two-handed scribbling – observe pupil at play and present work from the side he/she favours more for using a phone, telescope and kicking a ball – place a small whiteboard end-on to the pupil and get the pupil to draw patterns on both sides at same time (after a week the stronger side will usually appear).
Mark making – can the pupil: *Remember that children learn to imitate first then copy. Imitate = reproduce after a demonstration; Copy = reproduce from model* 	*Use a multi-sensory approach by selecting a range of activities taken from each of the sensory areas suggested below:*
☐ scribble to and fro holding pencil with palmar grasp? ☐ scribble and make dots holding pencil in pincer grasp?	*gross motor movement*: – play with cars and push-along toys; – wipe the table with damp cloth; swish hands in water and washing-up liquid to make bubbles;

Skill area to be checked:	If not, try the following activities:
☐ imitate vertical lines and sometimes V shapes?	– make ribbon patterns in the air – play marching games following the lines and direction of the desired pencil movement – encourage visual tracking (following a moving object from left to right) with motorised remote control toys.
☐ imitate horizontal line?	*visual stimuli*:
☐ imitate a circle?	– demonstrate movements in the air asking the pupil to imitate your actions
☐ imitate 'T' and 'V'?	– demonstrate mark making on white boards then ask the pupil to imitate your marks; when this is achieved move on to copying.
☐ draw horizontal and vertical lines?	*tactile (touch) stimuli*: – sand trays – lentil, pasta trays
☐ copy 'O V H T'?	– playdough (see Recipes) – finger paints (see Recipes) – shaving foam
☐ imitate 'X'?	– 'Roll 'n' Write' cards
☐ copy 'X O V H T'?	– use template to colour within a shape – use glue pens to form a raised outline for colouring within. *olfactory (smell) stimuli (check that the selected medium is child-friendly; exercise caution with essential oils)*:
☐ copy squares?	– use child-friendly scented crayons and markers
☐ copy triangles?	
☐ write a few letters spontaneously?	– use scented finger paints when providing tactile experiences – experiment with fruit and vegetable printing to reinforce mark making and left to right tracking. *auditory (sound) stimuli*: – use and reinforce directional language making sure the child understands when demonstrating up and down, forwards and backwards, over and under, left and right movements – use 'listen and do'-type CDs which reinforce listening skills and fine motor skills.

Skill area to be checked:	_If not, try the following activities:_

Drawing skills – can the pupil:

- ☐ draw a person with head and two more features?
- ☐ draw a person with head, trunk, legs and usually arms and fingers?
- ☐ draw a person with head, trunk, legs, arms, fingers and features?
- ☐ draw a house with windows, doors, roof and chimney?
- ☐ draw a recognisable house?
- ☐ draw pictures with several items and show an indication of background?
- ☐ colour pictures staying mainly within the lines?

Backward chaining/small-step approach: Break the task into a series of small steps. For example, when teaching how to draw a face:

- provide a series of drawings of faces with one feature missing
- ask the child to identify the missing feature
- demonstrate completion of the picture

- ask the child to complete the picture
- gradually increase the complexity of the task by removing prompts.

(The same model could be used for drawing a dog, cat, house.)

Bilateral integration – can the pupil (using two hands together sometimes, for different tasks):

- ☐ hold an object in two hands and perform an action?

- ☐ use one hand to steady an object while playing?

- ☐ hold an object in one hand while performing an action with the other?

- push a pram or a push-along toy
- hold steering wheel in toy car
- steer bike/trike by holding handle bars.
- inset jigsaws
- 'post' toys
- pretend and real baking (hold the bowl while stirring).
- peel a banana
- open a zip
- sharpen a pencil
- use a hairdryer and hairbrush together
- hold a cup while pouring water into it from a jug.

Skill area to be checked:	If not, try the following activities:
☐ pour a drink from a bottle into a cup without spilling? ☐ remove and replace a screw-top lid?	– pour and fill a container with marbles, pebbles, conkers, lentils, sand, water play – nut and bolt construction toys – café bar in home corner.

Crossing the midline

This is an important element of bi-manual integration (using two hands together). This can be encouraged using the activities on the right.	– dressing up games – dressing toys – sit cross-legged and pat opposite knee – march and touch opposite knee – cut food with knife and fork – Brain Gym, Activate activities – sort activities where objects have to be picked up with one hand and placed in a container at the other side.

Hand-eye co-ordination
– can the pupil:

☐ build a tower with 2 cubes following a demonstration? ☐ build a tower of 3 cubes following a demonstration (sometimes spontaneously)? ☐ build a tower of 6 or 7 cubes? ☐ build a tower of more than 7 bricks using the dominant hand? ☐ build a bridge using 3 bricks after a demonstration? ☐ build towers of more than 10 cubes? ☐ build bridges spontaneously using 3 bricks? ☐ build 3 steps using 6 cubes following a demonstration? ☐ thread a large needle? ☐ thread small beads?	– provide play opportunities with building blocks, starting with large lightweight blocks – provide a range of construction toys including self-adhesive varieties (Velcro/magnetic/interlocking) – gradually reduce the size of blocks/cubes – use modelling and demonstration techniques to encourage creativity – group pupils of differing abilities to provide positive role models. – provide a range of threading activities starting with dowel rods and progressing to stiffened cord and laces – provide a range of bodkins and needles so that the pupil can select equipment within his/her skill level thus ensuring success and reinforcing self-esteem.

66

Recipes for dough and finger paints

Playdough
1 part conditioner
2 parts cornflour
food colouring

Pour the cornflour into the
conditioner. Mix well. Add the food
colouring. Mix then use.
Textures such as sand, glitter could
be added.

Cornflour finger paint
Mix 2 cups of cornflour in a pan and
add water to make the consistency of
glue. Cook, stirring continuously until
it becomes a clear gel. Colour with
food colouring and cool.

Soap flakes finger paint
Combine soap flakes with sufficient
water to make a 'gluggy' texture. Mix
with an electric beater to achieve a
finger paint consistency. Add food
colouring.

Salt and flour finger paint
1 cup flour
4 tsp. salt
7/8 cups cold water

Combine flour, salt and water. Add
food colouring or paint. Mix well and
store in the fridge.

Part III

Strategies to address the educational implications of co-ordination difficulties

- Classroom activities
- Independence skills
- Communication and social skills
- Personal organisation

22 Classroom activities

This section offers advice and strategies on a range of topics related to developing recording skills. Much of the advice is based on existing good classroom practice, which can be observed in many mainstream schools.

The approaches suggested will benefit all pupils, not just those with co-ordination difficulties. Strategies are intended for use in the classroom but are also appropriate for use in small-group and individual settings.

Contents of this section:

- promoting a good sitting position for work;
- teaching handwriting, including cursive script;
- the procedure for assessing a pupil's writing;
- a classroom intervention following assessment;
- alternative recording strategies;
- teaching keyboard skills;
- teaching dictation skills;
- teaching cutting skills.

23 Sitting position for class activities

A poor sitting position results in a lack of stability for working. Weight is not equally distributed and muscles in one area are tenser than in others.

The brain has to concentrate on maintaining a stable sitting position, which results in complex fine motor activities such as writing becoming more difficult.

A good sitting position means sitting with:

- feet flat on the floor;
- bottom well back on the seat;
- back straight;
- head up and in the midline.

This provides a stable base and means that the hands can be used in bi-manual activities to the best effect.

Developing sitting balance at the Foundation Stage

To aid core stability and sitting balance, provide opportunities for pupils to draw/paint in a variety of positions, e.g.:

- prone or lying on tummy;
- standing at an easel or using a chalkboard;
- high kneeling;
- side leaning (resting on one elbow);
- on all fours.

This allows them to experience pressure on different areas of the body and helps to develop proprioception (see page 6).

This pupil is also sitting on a 'Movin' Sit' cushion, which tilts the pelvis forward resulting in a more upright position. This might prove beneficial for pupils who always sit with a rounded back, often as a consequence of low muscle tone.

The board angle can be between 20 and 45 degrees, depending on the pupil's needs. A number are available commercially, including the 'Writestart Desk' and the 'Write Angle'.

This pupil is using a 'Posture Pack', made up of a rubber wedged cushion and a large rigid file, with a carry handle, into which the wedge fits. A large lever arch file is a cheaper option if only an angled writing board is required.

When writing, the pupil also needs good shoulder, forearm, wrist and hand stability.

- Develop shoulder and forearm stability by encouraging pupils to draw with their elbows resting on the table.
- If there is a problem with wrist and hand stability, provide an angled board (below) on which the pupil can rest his/her forearms. Ask the pupil to rest the little-finger side of the working hand on the surface.

Remember to check that sitting position is correct when the pupil moves up through the school. In primary schools the size of furniture changes and pupils may be small or tall for their age. Therefore, seating should be reviewed at least annually.

A rough guide to the correct height for table and chairs is:

- tables should be half the pupil's height;
- chairs should be a third of the pupil's height;
- the pupil's forearms should rest comfortably on the desk and the shoulders should not be hunched .

Furniture of different sizes may be required in a classroom if there is a great difference in the height of pupils. This also applies if pupils are split up into ability groups for literacy and numeracy and move to different classrooms.

Adjustable height tables are available from a range of suppliers, e.g. Hope Education, Rompa, Vari-Tech Ltd, although they are fairly expensive. However, a few tables strategically placed in primary or in subject bases at secondary would fulfil most pupils' needs.

If it is not possible to provide lower tables and chairs, the pupil may require a foot block to support his/her feet to ensure stability (see left). For younger pupils, a toilet step from Ikea/Mothercare may be appropriate, or there are a number of commercially available wooden stacking foot blocks which provide a choice of heights (5, 7.5 and 10 cm). This allows the correct height of block to be used.

NB: If the pupil is under the supervision of a paediatric occupational therapist, always consult him/her if there are concerns about seating.

24 Teaching handwriting

Early years

- It is essential that pupils develop the correct formation from the start as bad habits are very difficult to break and cause problems with developing handwriting in the future.
- A child must have all the pre-skills in place before the teaching of letter formation begins, i.e. the ability to:

  - use the index finger in isolation;
  - hold objects in a pincer grasp;
  - hold a mark maker in a tripod grasp;
  - use finger and thumb in opposition;
  - demonstrate acceptable finger/hand strength;
  - rotate wrists and forearms.

- Pupils should be able to copy the following shapes before the teaching of letter formation:

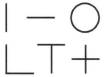

(NB: Children learn shapes in the following order:

- circle – 3 years;
- cross – 4 years 1 month;
- square – 4 years 6 months;
- triangle – 5 years 3 months.)

Activities to develop deficits in the above areas are described in the section 'Fine motor skill checklist and activities.

When the pupil can combine two letter elements he/she is ready to learn letter formation (see Progression of drawing skills in Appendix 3). Check readiness for writing by asking the pupil to copy the shapes in Appendix 3.

Teaching handwriting in Key Stage 1

Developing good handwriting is dependent on the pupil sitting correctly, having stability of the upper torso, shoulder, forearm and wrist, and a secure pencil grasp (page 62) which allows flexibility in the hand and wrist. Then:

- Ensure that the pupil has plenty of experience of gross motor movements and a secure understanding of directional speech, e.g. up, round, down, across, stop, start, circle, left, right, forwards, backwards, clockwise, anticlockwise; this reinforces letter formation (this may be incorporated into PE lessons, e.g. team games, maypole/country dancing, using ribbon sticks).
- Alongside this give the pupil opportunities for multi-sensory work in forming basic letter shapes in sand, paint, lentils, etc., as outlined in Mark making (page 63).
- Teach numbers first since there are fewer numbers than letters.
- For fluency to be achieved, it is important that the following are taught:
  - starting and finishing point;
  - flicks and tails;
  - clockwise and anticlockwise formation;
  - ascenders and descenders.
- Teach letter families together, e.g. 'c a d g q and o' (all starting with an anticlockwise circle); 'r n m h b and p' (all beginning with a downstroke), 'k v w x and z' (all involving diagonals), etc.
- Use an appropriate program on the interactive whiteboard which articulates the correct formation while demonstrating it.
- Encourage pupils to draw the letter in the air using their whole arm and join in with the verbal directions as they perform the action.
- Transfer the movement to paper once it is fully understood; encourage the pupil to continue to verbalise the movements while forming the letter.
- Provide lined paper – instructing the pupil to sit the letter on the line.
- Additionally, two or three minutes of hand exercises just before starting to write, e.g. stretching, clapping, shaking, fingertip presses, prepares muscles and increases hand and wrist strength and flexibility.

Generally, the school will have a handwriting policy which outlines the way handwriting is to be taught: whether flicks are taught right from the start, when script is introduced, whether lined paper is used, when writing with a pen is begun and what type of pen is used.

However, some pupils may need an individual approach which follows the school formula less rigidly – for example, for pupils who have poorly formed writing, using a fine biro gives better results than using a gel ink or ink pen. Biros have a 'drag' on the page, whereas gel ink pens flow freely and run away for some pupils.

Teaching cursive script

Cursive handwriting is made up of a small group of rhythmic movements, i.e.:

- long and short strokes (as in 'b, d, f, i, k, l, t' above the line and 'p, q' below the line and many capitals)

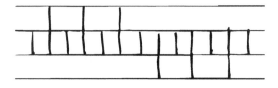

- push and pull garlands (as in 'h, n, m, r, u, y')

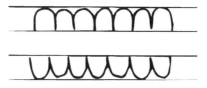

- clockwise and anticlockwise loops (loops below the line as in 'g, y f', and loops above the line as in 'e, f' and possibly others (depending on the school handwriting policy)

- clockwise ('b, p') and anticlockwise ('a, c, d, g, o, q') circles; to form a cursive 'c' ask the pupil to make waves, which sit on the line

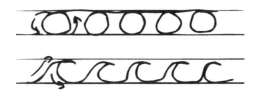

- zigzags ('k, q, w, v, z' and possibly 'y' depending on handwriting policy)

Pupils who have been taught to add 'flicks and tails' when printing letters should find these patterns relatively easy to copy. If necessary, allow pupils to practise forming them on the board using a whole-arm movement. NB: Up/down, etc., will have more relevance on a vertical surface and using the whole arm encourages the development of fluency.

These patterns will help to promote writing fluency. Many of these movements could also be included in PE, e.g. weaving through obstacles, or dance within a story setting. Performing these actions to music also helps establish fluency of movement.

Lined paper should be used with an intermediate line, if necessary, for writing practice. The teaching of 'flicks' should have established the connections between letters, but certain joins may need to be taught specifically since a number of pupils have real difficulty understanding where one letter starts and the next one begins, e.g.:

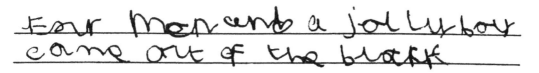

Aged 7 years

Note that the 'ou' in the first word 'Four' is made up of a clockwise 'o' and poorly joined 'ur', the 'm' in 'came' has no initial downstroke, and the movements for the letters and joins required in the combinations for 'out' and 'ack' in 'black' are not understood at all (see page 89 for recommended intervention for this pupil).

Some schools teach cursive script right from the start, generally with great success. This establishes correct letter formation and the pupils learn to write only once. It also aids spelling since the hand learns the pattern of the word. However, opinions differ, so the decision to implement it or not must be left to the management team of each school.

Strategies to counter lack of improvement

If a multi-sensory approach to teaching handwriting is begun at the Foundation Stage and the child has moved through and achieved the hierarchical pre-writing skills of mark making, shape copying, combining letter elements and basic letter formation, writing should progress well. However, by Key Stages 1 and 2 problems may well be established.

Sometimes a highly structured programme of PE exercises (rather than frequent repetition of practising, or redrafting, writing), involving the development of hand-eye co-ordination, balance, spatial awareness and fine motor skill activities, e.g. accurate throwing and catching of balls/beanbags, may result in improved writing – and be seen as 'fun'.

Performance improves for a number of reasons: increased skill level, raised self-esteem and confidence, better working relationships with staff and greater motivation to persevere.

In addition, assess handwriting using the forms provided in Appendix 4 and, if appropriate, put intervention strategies in place.

25 Assessing handwriting

When assessing a sample of handwriting, observe how the pupil works, e.g.:

- Does the pupil have a good working posture?
- Is he/she tense, does he/she hold his/her breath or use an unusual pencil grip?
- Check the position of the wrist – is it stiff and/or slightly hooked?

When observing the pupil writing, note:

- problems with formation of letters, e.g. clockwise 'o's;
- reversals (left to right or top to bottom);
- erratic sizing of letters;
- age-appropriate sizing, larger/smaller;
- alignment – does writing sit on the line/follow the margin?
- spacing – lack of/erratic;
- is writing laborious; does speed of production decrease after a short period?
- are mixed upper- and lower-case letters seen?
- is perseveration seen, e.g. not knowing when to stop when forming a circle?

For early writers, use sample of handwriting sheets 1 and/or 2

Assess the pupil by asking him/her to:

- draw a picture of a person;
- write his/her name;
- copy or write the alphabet;
- copy or free write a short sentence.

For independent writers, use sample of handwriting sheets 3 and/or 4

Assess the pupil by asking him/her to:

- copy the following sentence:

Four men and a jolly boy came out of the black and pink house quickly to see the bright violet sun but the sun was behind a cloud.

- also copy or free write to dictation:

the quick brown fox jumps over the lazy dog

Use the assessment form (Appendix 4) to record problems noted.

26 Interventions following assessment

Systematic response

When the assessment form is completed, go through it point by point.

The numbers below correspond to those on the assessment sheet. Numbers 1 to 5 are prerequisites and must be corrected before handwriting can be addressed.

1. Seating position for handwriting

The pupil should be in a good sitting position (see Chapter 23), with feet flat and bottom to the back of the seat to provide a stable base and fix the trunk.

- Provide a fixed angled board or foot block to improve writing position, if required.
- Seat the pupil appropriately within the classroom (Classroom organisation – page 26).

2. Handedness

Left-handers need particular attention to ensure that they can both see their work and develop a suitable grip. Sit left-handers next to one another, or place them to the left of right-handers, to ensure that the writing arm is free.

3. Angling the paper

Angle the paper to the right or left depending on handedness – this reduces tension in the writing arm.

Left-handers should angle the paper to the right from 30 to 45 degrees as required. The paper should also be positioned slightly to the left of the body (see left).

For right-handers the paper should be angled 30 degrees to the left and positioned to the right of the body (see right).

4. Fixing

The pupil should hold the paper with his/her free hand to prevent the paper slipping. This helps to stabilise the trunk. For younger pupils use a visual prompt, e.g. stick an A4 piece of paper at the appropriate angle on the table top, with a cut-out of the free hand superimposed on it. Encourage a 'triangular' working position, with the head and the elbows making the triangle.

For older pupils, a line of coloured tape placed at the correct angle would be sufficient. If pupils are unable to fix the paper themselves, use Blu-tack, a rubberised non-slip mat or a clipboard.

5. Grasp

The standard tripod grip (right) is not always the most appropriate or comfortable for some pupils. As long as the grip is effective and relaxed, allow the pupil to use it.

It is generally possible to see if the grip is not effective, since the pencil will appear to be clenched in the hand.

Tension may also be seen in the wrist, which is rigid and sometimes slightly hooked, resulting in stiff, spiky writing, which is erratically sized, lacking in fluency.

Tense grips

 If the pupil rolls his/her thumb over the index finger (left), the grip is generally tense and insecure.

Likewise, the pupil who holds his/her pencil along the barrel (right) will generally have difficulty gaining fluency.

The hooked wrist position is often used by left-handers since it allows them to see what is being written. When seen in right-handers, it is generally due to poor proprioceptive feedback (see page 6) from the wrist, elbow and shoulder. Both should be changed if possible. A weak grasp, which the pupil is constantly readjusting, should also be changed.

82

Changing a pencil grip

Often a moulded grip such as the 'Crossguard' or 'Ultra' grip, which requires the pupil to position his/her fingers correctly, proves beneficial (see right).

These pencil grips are most suitable for primary-aged pupils.

Secure grips that can be tried are the four-fingered grip (similar to the tripod grip but using the ring finger as well) and the 'Monk's' grip (holding the pen between the index and middle fingers), illustrated left. Older pupils adapt to this grip well.

Additionally, have available a range of pencil grips as well as pencils with different-sized barrels (including maxi and triangular) for pupils to try.

For older pupils try the 'Tri-go' grip (left), the small 'Stubbi' or 'Stetro' grip (middle) and the 'Grip it' (right). The 'Handiwriter' (not shown) is a similar writing aid which attaches to the pencil above and below the thumb.

However, some older pupils may be too embarrassed to use a moulded grip. In this case use Blu-tack moulded to shape, or wrap one or two rubber bands around the barrel of the pencil at the usual holding position. Some pens now have integral rubber grips, which may prove sufficient.

Have available a range of pens for pupils to try. Include gel ink pens as well as ball-points in the assessment kit, some with rubberised grips, since they each have a different 'feel' and what suits one pupil may not suit another.

Always ensure that the pen/pencil is not held too close to the end of the barrel since this can obscure work.

6. Too much or too little pressure

Training the proprioceptors (sensors in the joints) in the upper limbs will help, e.g.:

- ask the pupil to do 10 to 15 chair (or desk) 'press-ups' prior to writing activities;
- organise a paper 'sandwich' with carbon paper between:

    - for pupils who apply too much pressure, ask them *not* to mark the bottom paper (start with three sheets to allow them to observe gradual improvement);
    - for pupils who apply too little pressure, ask them to ensure that the carbon paper *is* marked;

- alternatively, raise the desk or provide an angled board for pupils whose pressure is too light on the paper and lower the desk for those who press too hard;
- prepare the muscles involved by doing two to three minutes of hand exercises before all writing activities, e.g.:

    - shake, flap or rotate hands; 10 fingertip presses;
    - clench fists and release × 10;
    - walk fingertips along the desk;
    - touch thumb to each finger as quickly as possible;
    - finger rhymes such as 'Here's the Church, Here's the Steeple …';

- provide a softer pencil/fibre tip pen for pupils who apply light pressure.

7. Incorrect formation

- A pattern may be noted when looking at which letters were incorrectly formed by the pupil during the assessment, e.g. clockwise 'o's (which will impede the development of cursive script) used for 'a, g, o', etc.:

    - a gross motor programme concentrating on moving to speech directions would help the pupil to understand the difference between clockwise and anticlockwise;
    - also teach the movements required for that particular family of letters again (see page 76);

- The letters 'k' and 'x' involve diagonals and how they are formed will indicate whether the pupil has difficulties crossing the midline of the body (see pages 46 and 54);
- Also check if the pupil can copy flowing letter patterns.

84

8. Reversals

Often, pupils with mixed laterality, i.e. right-handed but left-eye dominant, have problems with developing left/right orientation on the page, reversals of letters or words and mixing left/right sides of the body.

Check for cross-laterality and note down:

- which hand the pupil writes with;
- which foot he/she kicks with;
- which eye he/she uses to look through a telescope;
- which ear he/she uses to answer the phone.

For letter/number reversals, use a multi-sensory approach, e.g.:

- motor – draw the letter/number shape on the floor placing a green beanbag at the starting place and a red beanbag indicating where to stop; ask the pupil to walk around the shape while vocalising the movements;
- touch – write letter/number on the pupil's back and ask him/her to guess what it is;
- sight – use three-dimensional letters and ask the pupil to finger-trace;
- auditory – encourage the pupil to verbalise the movements as he/she forms letters.

9. Erratic sizing

Use lined paper with additional guidelines for ascenders and descenders. Triple-lined pages; or books, are available to purchase.

10. Alignment

If alignment is poor and work gradually wanders to the right of the page, use the traffic light system to aid setting out work, i.e.:

- put a green dot at the left side of the page to indicate 'start here';
- put a red dot at the right side of the page to indicate 'do not write beyond this spot';
- if necessary, put an orange dot 2 cm before the red dot to indicate 'do not begin a long word beyond this point'.

11. Spacing

To assist spacing, provide a paper, or card, word 'spacer'. The pupil may also use his/her finger to separate words.

NB: Areas 7, 8, 10 and 11 are most effectively addressed in the long term by using a structured perceptuo-motor programme, e.g. 'Write from the Start', which focuses on each skill area involved. This is worked through as a whole for younger pupils. However, occasionally, older pupils' specific problems may be improved by working through two or three of the booklets – the Teacher's Manual lists the emphasis of each booklet. Be aware, however, that some exercises are not age-appropriate for secondary pupils.

12. *Fluency/speed*

- Normal writing speed varies depending on the context, but progresses from an average of 1.5 words per minute at age five to 18 words per minute at 16 (see sample of handwriting sheets 3 and 4 in Appendix 4).
- Writing speed should be checked before any intervention, then at least annually.
- To request special arrangements in exams the teacher must have up-to-date information regarding a pupil's speed of writing over a period of time.

Slant

It is now accepted that slant of writing should be according to individual preference.

If a pupil is following a handwriting programme, do not insist on a similar slant to the model. It is correct formation that is the major concern in the development of a fluent script.

Assessment pack

Put together an assessment pack and have available:

- a selection of pencils, e.g. thin, chubby or triangular barrels, soft lead/hard lead;
- different pencil grips: triangular, soft foam, 'Crossguard', 'Ultra', 'Tri-go', 'Stretro' or 'Stubbi' moulded grips, 'Handiwriter', etc.;
- a good selection of pens available for the pupil to try, e.g. 'Stabilo S Move' pens and pencils, pens with triangular or rubber grips, 'gel' or biro pens – generally available from good art shops;
- angled boards/large lever arch file (the cheap option to use as an angled board at secondary level)/Posture Pack, etc.;
- foot blocks of different heights (5, 7.5 and 10 cm) available to try if required;
- lined paper, including additional lines for guidance with ascenders and descenders;
- 'Speed Up' from LDA by Lois Addy (a book of exercises to help pupils build up fluency and writing speed).

27 Handwriting samples

Sample 1

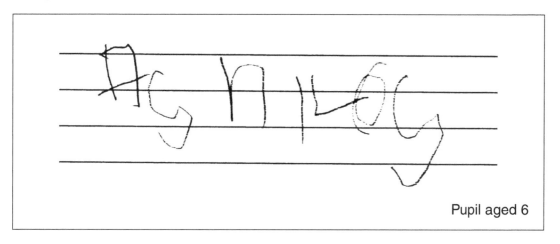

Pupil aged 6

A pupil with significant fine motor co-ordination difficulties demonstrating the following:

- a weak two-fingered pencil grip;
- he could combine two letter elements (therefore ready to begin writing) and produce an approximation of his name;
- he was unable to draw a triangle (cross the midline);
- he was at a very early stage of writing.

Recommended intervention:

- to develop finger/hand strength – fingertip presses, popping bubble wrap, squeezing out sponges, making plasticine/clay models, etc.;
- provide an 'Ultra' pencil grip and work on developing a secure grasp;
- provide a fixed-angled board so the pupil can see work more easily (also improves pressure on paper);
- work on gross motor activities to reinforce letter formation and language of movement, e.g. letters on the floor in the hall (chalk or rope), the pupil walks around the shape describing movement; then teach letter families;
- to learn orientation of letters draw a letter on his back and ask him to guess what it is (develops orientation to his own body);

- work on crossing the midline (gross and fine motor);
- use 'Write from the Start' to develop perceptuo-motor skills;
- use alternative means of recording work to demonstrate ability;
- develop keyboard skills (to provide an alternative means of recording work).

Sample 2

Pupil aged 7

A statemented pupil with a number of medical problems demonstrating the following:

- the pupil held the pencil with fingers arranged along the barrel, therefore limiting control ('Ultra' grip provided);
- he could cross the midline, but note problems with reversals ('s, z'); 'a, g, o, q' were produced using clockwise 'o's;
- erratic sizing of letters with 'p, g, q' standing on the line, mixed upper- and lower-case;
- copying flowing letter patterns – he began well, but could not sustain the fluid movement required due to a stiff, slightly hooked wrist.

Recommended intervention:

- work on gross motor movements for problem letters, i.e. where letters begin and end ('s, z', clockwise and anticlockwise letters);
- teach the 'o' letter family ('a, c, d, g, q, o') at the same time, followed by other letter families;
- follow a programme of activities to strengthen and improve flexibility in wrists, e.g. turning skipping rope, ribbon sticks, stir cakes at home;

- draw flowing letter patterns using the pen tools on the interactive whiteboard (as large as possible and ask him to reduce the size);
- use apps on the iPad to improve letter formation;
- to learn orientation of letters, draw a letter on his back and ask him to guess what it is (develops orientation to his own body);
- use 'Write from the Start' to develop perceptuo-motor skills;
- develop keyboard skills (to provide an alternative means of recording work).

Sample 3

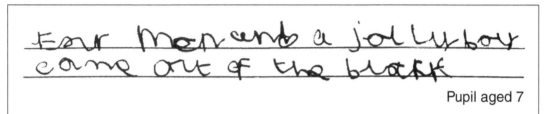

Pupil aged 7

A Year 3 pupil demonstrating the following:

- a secure four-fingered grip;
- he fixed with his free hand, but did not angle the paper;
- he could copy 2D shapes, but had problems with 3D shapes;
- he produced a cursive script, but did not understand the correct formation of some letters, e.g. 'o, a, d' (clockwise formation); however, note the 'o' in 'jolly' and 'boy' is correctly formed;
- he also had problems with 'd/b' (testing positive for cross-laterality);
- 'j, y' were above the line (no descenders);
- writing was erratic in sizing and spacing;
- his writing lacked fluency, but was age-appropriate for speed of production of work (28 letters per minute).

Recommended intervention:
- provide a template of writing position on his desk (indicating how much to angle the paper);
- strengthen hands and fingers, e.g. squeezing out sponges in the bath, helping to wring out face cloths, popping bubble wrap, etc.;
- draw flowing letter patterns on the interactive whiteboard (as large as possible to begin with and gradually reduce in size);
- draw lines of upper, middle and lower planes for guidance when practising ascenders and descenders – on the whiteboard first, then on paper;
- some parts of 'Write from the Start', i.e. dealing with fluency, sizing and spacing;
- draw letter on the pupil's back and ask him to guess what it is (develops orientation to his own body);
- teach keyboard skills (to provide an alternative means of recording work).

Sample 4

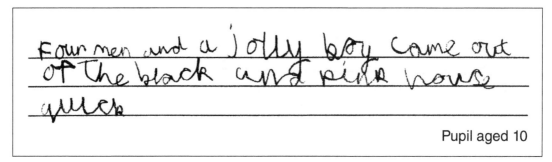

Four men and a jolly boy came out of the black and pink house quick

Pupil aged 10

This pupil was being screened for dyslexia and was suspected of having scotopic sensitivity. He demonstrated the following:

- a secure tripod grip, did not angle the paper, but fixed with his free hand;
- he reported that he found white paper 'glaring';
- he tested positive for cross-laterality;
- he had no problem copying 2D and 3D shapes – could cross the midline and had a good awareness of spatial concepts;
- fluency of writing was developing (53 letters per minute, which is age-appropriate), but some erratic sizing was noted; however, spacing was good;
- formation was good apart from 'f, x';
- some descenders sat on the line, e.g. 'p, j'.

Recommended intervention:

- the provision of a line of tape on his desk (to show how to angle the paper);
- write on alternate lines to reduce visual clutter;
- use pastel-coloured paper (to reduce glare);
- staff should be aware of the possible problems associated with cross-laterality;
- he should work on some parts of 'Write from the Start', i.e. dealing with fluency;
- the provision of upper, middle and lower planes for guidance when practising ascenders and descenders – whiteboard first, then on paper;
- practise to improve formation of 'f, x' to enable him to form links correctly.

Sample 5

The quick brown fox jumps over the lazy dog !.

Pupil aged 10

A Year 6 pupil with a hemiplegia, very motivated, who had worked very hard to develop a fluent cursive script. However, speed of work production decreased over time.

> **Recommended intervention:**
>
> - that the pupil develops touch typing skills;
> - the provision of support for recording work at secondary school.

28 Alternative recording strategies

Some pupils find recording in a conventional manner to be problematic and alternatives need to be considered.

Maths

- The pupil solves the problem, points to the number on a number line and the adult writes the answer.
- Stickers with pre-written numbers are available for the pupil to peel off and stick onto his/her book, when he/she has completed the problem.
- Use number stamps to allow the pupil to put the answers onto his/her worksheet, book.
- Use computer programs to record work, e.g. '2simple Maths City' (younger pupils to Year 6).
- A lack of ability to record numbers should not impede the development of maths skills – thus, access to ICT is essential.

Written tasks

- The younger pupil could produce a number of name labels on the computer, which he/she can stick onto paintings etc. without having to struggle to write.
- The adult writes at the pupil's dictation.
- The pupil records a sentence/story and the adult transcribes.
- Cloze procedure, which can take a variety of forms:
  - sentences with a choice of words to circle, to allow the pupil to demonstrate his/her knowledge;
  - the pupil is given information prepared by the teacher, in a pictorial or written form; the pupil fills in gaps (in pictorial or word form) in order to demonstrate what knowledge he/she has acquired.
  - the pupil circles the word, copies the word or sticks a pre-written word in the space.

Goldilocks   **baby bear**

.... was in bed.

- Use individual word banks containing key words the pupil can read plus words linked to classroom work, the words attached with Velcro. The pupil composes the sentence, finds the words and attaches them to a Velcro strip. Matching words can then be available for the pupil to stick into his/her workbook if writing is difficult.
- Use the Clicker program with key words programmed into a grid to support specific subject areas, e.g. history, geography. These can be purchased or downloaded.
- Use software such as '2simple 2Create a Story' (www.2simple.com).
- Give multi-choice questions which allow the pupil to circle the correct answer.
- Provide opportunities for collaborative working in which another pupil scribes the ideas of the group.
- Try voice recognition programs such as 'Dragon Naturally Speaking' (available as an app).
- Use ICT to allow the pupil to produce more attractive pieces of work, which can be illustrated using images from the internet, thereby overcoming poor drawing skills. It may be useful to teach touch typing skills to some pupils.
- Scanning of worksheets etc., which can be adapted, would allow the pupil to fill in the gaps to demonstrate levels of knowledge.
- Consideration should be given to how pupils with poor recording skills might make the notes they need to read back for revision, e.g.:

  - dictaphones,
  - teacher notes to be made accessible,
  - PowerPoint notes given,
  - photocopying of a peer's notes to be allowed.

- It may be useful to teach dictation skills to some pupils (see Chapter 31).
- Avoid copying from the board, provide PowerPoint notes instead.
- To overcome poor drawing skills, use stencils to create diagrams, or use pre-drawn diagrams for the pupil to label.

29 Teaching keyboard skills

Pupils with delayed writing skills should have access to ICT equipment; this provides an alternative to handwriting, requiring minimal physical input, and enables the production of work that looks age-appropriate.

Most pupils use the 'hunt and peck' method when typing. However, if keyboard skills are to be an effective alternative to writing, they need to be taught in a structured way, building up skills hierarchically. There are a number of pre-skills required:

- the pupil must have good sitting balance in order to use hands together;
- he/she must be able to isolate fingers (at least the index finger) on both hands.

If the pupil has effective use of one limb only, he/she must be able to stabilise the trunk with the weaker limb and isolate the index finger of the dominant hand.

With younger pupils, teaching the ability to write their names is motivating and teaches the placement of between ten and 15 letters on the keyboard, as well as the function keys, space, return and backspace (delete). For example, if the pupil is called Robert, the first letter is pointed out on the keyboard with the instruction to press the 'r' and then the space bar, to make a block of letters:

r r r r r r r r r r r r r r r r r r r r
r r r r r r r r r r r r r r r r r r r r

The pupil does not need to understand the difference between capitals and lower-case; he is simply pressing a key with the first letter of his name. However, in reality Robert is learning a whole range of skills:

- the sound 'r' has two symbols: 'R' and 'r';
- the space bar is used to separate letters and eventually words;
- backspace is used to make corrections and the return key to move down;
- discipline, to produce work accurately (since only accuracy is rewarded by a print-out to take home).

The use of the 'caps' key is not important at this stage; just continue to teach the pupil to type his name one letter at a time:

ro ro ro ro ro ro ro ro ro ro
ro ro ro ro ro ro ro ro ro ro

then:

rob rob rob rob rob rob rob, etc.

NB: Saying the letter out loud as it is pressed reinforces the action. Also, the pupil should be using the correct finger for the left or right side of the keyboard, so 'r' is pressed with the left index finger and 'o' is pressed with the right index finger.

When the first name has been learned, the surname can be taught in the same way. Once he/she can type both names accurately, teach the use of the caps key, or how to operate the shift key with the other hand, since this is more time efficient.

Limit the amount of practice time to 5–10 minutes per day, to prevent boredom. Providing a printout usually maintains motivation.

When appropriate, proceed to teaching key words, e.g. mum, dad, cat, dog. In addition, words from reading/spelling lists can be used to reinforce placement of letters, as well as improve access times, e.g.:

the the the the the the the the the
the the the the the the the the the

For older pupils it would be more appropriate to use high frequency words, including some subject-specific vocabulary for typing practice. Use the same method as above and limit practice to 10–15 minutes per day.

Additional considerations:

- If necessary, use a card 'mask' over the keyboard and cut out the letters one at a time as they are introduced. Remember to cut out gaps for the space bar and return key, to reduce the distraction of other keys and improve concentration on the task.
- Occasionally, co-ordination is so poor that the pupil needs a keyguard, which may be used with/without a mask, as appropriate.
- Raising the back of the keyboard or using an angled board can help the pupil see the keys more clearly.
- Use a standard word processing package unless the pupil needs auditory feedback to reinforce letter sounds and aid spelling. Many classrooms have 'Talking First Word', or a useful alternative is 'Write:Outloud'. 'First Keys 2' also supports the English curriculum and helps to develop keyboard skills.
- If the pupil has problems with the auto-repeat feature, switch it off from the Settings menu (*Control Panel – Keyboard – Speed*).

Teaching touch typing

Once the pupil is a proficient two-finger typist and if writing is still developing slowly or there are problems with either legibility or production of work, consider the option of teaching them to touch type.

Advantages

The pupil:

- can achieve higher speeds of typing with motivation and practice (over 40 wpm);
- does not have to look repeatedly from screen to keyboard;
- can type from text/notes/whiteboard with greater ease;
- learns the *pattern* of words with fingers on the keyboard (in the same way that the hand learns the pattern when you develop cursive script, aiding spelling);
- learns a transferable skill with possibly greater opportunities in workplace.

Disadvantages

Pupils have to:

- learn to use all fingers with equal dexterity;
- learn which fingers match which keys;
- persevere with exercises which may appear boring since it takes some time to develop accuracy and speed.

Pre-skills

Staff need to check that pupils can:

- isolate each finger – can the pupil touch each finger to thumb?
- understand the movements up, down, left/right, etc., in relation to the keyboard.

Method

- Use the same principles as mentioned in teaching two-fingered typing, i.e. short teaching sessions and printouts, to maintain motivation.
- The aim is reasonable proficiency in producing work; complete accuracy may not be achieved, or even achievable.
- Learning to touch type requires a degree of commitment and an understanding that it takes time for the skill to become automatic.

Consider the following resources:

1. 'Speedy Keys' (Inclusive Technology) – structured keyboard activities that are fun
2. 'First Keys to Literacy' (Widgit Software) – developing keyboard skills through literacy activities
3. 'English Type Junior' (demonstration version available from www.englishtype.com) – suitable for pupils with special educational needs
4. 'Five Finger Typist' (Inclusive Technology) is for pupils who can only use one hand
5. '2simple 2Type'

There are also a number of programs for developing typing skills which are free to download from the internet, e.g.:

1. FreeTypingGame.Net
2. Dance Mat Typing (www.BBC.co.uk/schools/typing)

30 Early keyboard skills checklist

Name: .... DOB: ....

Skill	Begun	Mastered	Programs used
1. Understands cause and effect (e.g. programs using space bar)			
2. Types first name unaided			
3. Uses space bar/return and delete key			
4. Uses number line			
5. Uses number line/return and space bar			
6. Uses arrow keys			
7. Types full name unaided			
8. Uses caps lock/shift key			
9. Copy types a sentence			
10. Uses full stop			
11. Speed increasing			
Mouse skills			
1. Can single-click on a large object			
2. Draws simple picture using shapes			
3. Can single-click on a small object			
4. Produces more detailed picture			
5. Can 'click and drag' in a program			
6. Can 'click and drag' on the desktop			
7. Can double-click			
Computer control			
1. Can switch on and log on			
2. Can switch off correctly			

Skill	Begun	Mastered	Programs used
3. Can open own folder of work			
4. Can select and open programs			
Keyboard shortcuts and use of menus			

1. Can print own work
   a. using Ctrl + P
   b. using Print from menu bar			

2. Can save work
   a. Ctrl + S
   b. from menu bar			

3. Can open a new file
   a. Ctrl + 0
   b. from menu bar			

4. Can quit from the program
   a. Alt + F4
   b. from the menu bar			

5. Can 'select all' text
   a. Ctrl + A
   b. from the Edit menu			

6. Can change font (Font menu)			
7. Can highlight text using click & drag			

8. Can format work selecting
   a. **bold** (Ctrl + B)
   b. *italic* (Ctrl + I)
   c. underline (Ctrl + U)			

9. Can change font size
   a. from font bar
   b. Ctrl + Shift + > or <			

10. Can use Ctrl + C to copy text			
11. Can use Ctrl + V to paste text			
12. Can use Ctrl + X to delete text			

13. Can create new folder
   a. from right-hand click menu
   b. Ctrl + N			

14. Can save work to own folder			
15. Can 'save as' using F12 key			
16. Can close window using Ctrl + W			
17. Can use Ctrl + Z to undo			

31 Teaching dictation skills

For some pupils, e.g. those with severe dyspraxia/dyslexia or those whose written work does not reflect their level of knowledge, a means of recording work may be by dictation. This is especially important for those approaching examinations at secondary level.

Dictating work, whether to a support assistant or using word recognition software, requires a level of skill, experience and self-discipline. It is important that the support assistant does not anticipate the answer, extending or improving sentences, since the aim is to provide evidence of the pupil's level of attainment.

Additionally, to get good grades in examinations, pupils need to show the planning of an essay, since this can add marks if there is insufficient time to finish a question.

Pupils need to develop a series of skills in the following sequence:

Stage:	To move to the next stage:
The pupil dictates: ☐ short phrases ☐ longer phrases with 'and' links ☐ grammatically correct short sentences ☐ longer grammatically correct sentences with one linking word, e.g. and, but, however, although ☐ sentences, showing how to indicate 'new sentence', 'full stop', 'comma', 'new paragraph'.	• discuss redrafting and ask 'who did what?', 'when/where/why?' • go over work and ask pupil to break it up into shorter sentences based on the above • use set/created Clicker grids to demonstrate links and sentence structure • use 'story starts' and picture sequences to extend sentences • read the pupil's work back and ask him/ her to note breath pauses (full stop) and shorter pauses (comma), make it a game • give the pupil a passage with no punctuation and ask him/her to punctuate.
Planning answers – can the pupil: ☐ sequence a series of sentences describing an activity? ☐ identify the beginning, middle and end of a story? ☐ plan a short story by giving main points, written on Post-its, and organising these into an answer?	• use set/prepared Clicker grids • give longer passages which have been cut up and ask the pupil to sequence them • use software, e.g. 'Kidspiration' or '2simple'.

32 Teaching scissor skills

Prerequisites

The pupil must be able to:

- open and close the hand;
- use both hands together, with the dominant hand leading and the other hand assisting;
- isolate or combine the movements of thumb, index and middle fingers;
- co-ordinate arm, hand and eye movements;
- stabilise the wrist, elbow and shoulder joints to provide a base for hand movements;
- show evidence of imitating cutting movements in play situations.

Pre-scissors activities	
Pick-up games Resources: • a bucket or container • salad servers, sugar tongs, etc. • a variety of small objects, e.g. cotton/aluminium foil balls, plastic toys, bells, bricks.	Objectives: • the pupil has to pick up objects and carry them to the bucket/container • gradually increase the distance.
Squeeze play Resources: • squirt guns, bulb-squeezers, turkey basters, etc. • balloons, washing-up liquid.	Objectives: • the pupil has to squirt water into a bowl of soapy water to make bubbles • the pupil has to squirt water at balloons hanging from a line to make them move.
Paper-punch games Resources: • paper punch • stiff paper/thin card • laces/crayons.	Objectives: • the pupil makes random holes in the paper/card with the punch and then joins the holes with laces/crayon marks • draw a path on a piece of card and ask the pupil to punch holes along the path.

Activities such as scrunching tissue/thin/thick paper, tearing it into random pieces then strips, etc. also help to develop bi-manual hand control.

Holding the scissors correctly:

- The pupil should place the thumb and middle fingers through the scissor loops.
- The index finger stabilises the scissors resting just above the lower loop (see right).

Simplifying the cutting task

To teach cutting along a straight line – ask the pupil to:

- cut along a line of punched holes (reducing task into a series of small snips);
- cut between two lolly sticks stuck on the paper;
- cut along the edge of a piece of card stuck on the paper;
- cut through the middle of a line of small stickers on the paper;
- cut along a line drawn with a thick marker pen.

To teach cutting out a circle – ask the pupil to:

- cut around a circle of punched holes;
- cut around the edge of a round piece of card stuck on the paper;
- cut out the circle in sections (the template looks like a radiating sun);
- cut around a circle of small stickers on the paper;
- cut around a circle drawn with a thick marker pen.

Resources

Low muscle tone/limited physical ability may result in poor scissor skills. The main difficulty is opening the scissors blades once they are closed. Scissors are available which reduce this problem. All the self-opening scissors shown below have safety caps in place.

Types of scissors	Comments	
Foundation Stage Fiskars Nursery 'Squeezer' Small 'Easy Grip' Fiskars Safety	• snipping action only • single loop requiring squeeze action • plastic blades	

KS1 and KS2
Teaching scissors
(right- or left-handed)
'Easy Grip'
 	
Right- and left-handed
self-opening
Long loop right- and
left-handed self-opening
Long loop right- and
left-handed (not shown)
Fiskars Junior right- and
left-handed
	• two holes in each handle
	
	• single loop requiring
	  squeeze action
	• spring-loaded action
	
	• all four fingers used in lower
	  grip
	• all four fingers used in lower
	  grip
	• larger lower loop

33 Scissor skills checklist

Stage	Developmental stage	Date achieved
1.	The pupil shows an interest in scissors	
2.	The pupil holds and manipulates scissors appropriately	
3.	The pupil opens and closes scissors in a controlled fashion	
4.	The pupil makes random snips	
5.	The pupil manipulates the scissors in a forward motion	
	✂ cuts across a 2 cm strip of thin card in any fashion	
	✂ cuts across a 5 cm strip of thin card in any fashion	
	✂ cuts across a 10 cm strip of thin card in any fashion	
	✂ cuts across a 20 cm strip of thin card in any fashion	
6.	The pupil begins to control the forward movement of the scissors	
	✂ cuts across paper, staying within a 15 cm line	
	✂ cuts across paper, staying within a 10 cm line	
	✂ cuts across paper, staying within a 5 cm line	
	✂ cuts across paper, staying within a 2 cm line	
7.	The pupil cuts along a straight line accurately	
	✂ cuts along a thick line made with a marker pen	
	✂ cuts along a thinner line made with a marker pen	
8.	The pupil cuts simple geometric shapes	
	✂ cuts out a square or oblong	
	✂ cuts out a triangle	
	✂ cuts out a semicircle	
	✂ cuts out a circle	
9.	The pupil cuts out simple figure shapes	

Stage	Developmental stage	Date achieved
10.	The pupil cuts out complex figure shapes	
11.	The pupil cuts non-paper materials	

Date begun: ....

Comments: ....

....

....

....

34　Independence skills

9 months	• holds, bites, chews small pieces of food • puts hands around bottle or cup when feeding • tries to grasp spoon when being fed.
1 year	• drinks from cup with little assistance • holds spoon and attempts to use for feeding (very messy) • helps with dressing by holding out arm for sleeve, foot for shoe.
15 months	• holds a cup and drinks without assistance • holds spoon, brings to mouth and licks it but unable to stop it turning over • chews well • helps with dressing.
18 months	• holds spoon, gets food safely to mouth but may still play with food • lifts and holds cup in both hands, drinks independently but hands empty cup to adult • assists with dressing, takes off own hat, shoes and socks but seldom able to replace • indicates urgent toilet needs by restlessness and vocalisation • bowel control may be attained but variable • may indicate wet or soiled nappy/pants.
2 years	• eats independently with a spoon but is easily distracted • puts on hat and shoes • usually attempts to say toilet needed in sufficient time, still unreliable.
2½ years	• eats skilfully with a spoon and may use a fork • pulls pants down when using the toilet but seldom able to replace them • may be dry through the night but this is variable.
3 years	• washes hands but needs help with drying • can eat with a spoon and sometimes a fork • can pull pants up and down, needs help with fastenings • is clean and dry in the day, almost reliable at night (variable).

4 years	• eats skilfully with spoon and fork
	• dresses, undresses independently apart from laces, ties, back buttons
	• can wipe own bottom
	• can wash and dry hands.
5 years	• eats competently using a knife and fork
	• dresses and undresses independently
	• washes and dries hands and face but needs supervision for the rest.

Reference

Adapted from Sheridan, M. (2003) *From Birth to Five Years*, Routledge.

35 Developing self-help skills

Dressing skills

- Encourage the pupil to use a long mirror. Play games to develop awareness of body size and shape.
- Develop movements for putting clothes on, e.g. quoits over wrists, ankles and hoops up to the waist and over the head, before practising dressing skills.
- Play games to practise skills, e.g. dressing up with large clothes in the house corner.
- Backward chaining would be a useful method to teach the putting on of items of clothing, e.g. putting on trousers:

    - help pupil put trousers on up to knees; pupil pulls the trousers up independently;
    - help pupil put trousers on up to ankles; pupil pulls trousers up independently;
    - help pupil put one leg in; pupil continues;
    - pupil is shown how to lay trousers out and put them on;
    - pupil sits and puts trousers on independently.

- Practise doing fasteners on dolls which have large buttons, zips and Velcro fastenings, do laces on wooden shoeboxes or tie up parcels.
- Encourage parents to dress their child in shoes with Velcro fastenings, trousers/ skirts with elasticated waist, school ties on elastic, clothes which are not tight (it may be necessary for uniform to have modifications to accommodate this).
- Younger pupils may benefit from having all their belongings, bags, hats in a particular colour, in order for them to be found more easily in the cloakroom.
- Provide cue cards or lists to show what order clothes are taken off/put on.

| Trousers | T-shirt | Trainers | Jumper |

- Encourage sitting to dress/undress, sitting with the back to a solid surface or holding onto a chair back to aid balance.
- Use T-shirts/sweatshirts with a logo/design on the front to help orientation of clothes.
- Give praise for effort when the pupil is trying to dress independently.
- Only help the pupil when he/she has tried for him-/herself.
- Ensure the pupil does not miss out on playtime etc. if he/she is slow to dress.

Older pupils

- Older pupils need to develop coping strategies to overcome their difficulties.
- Clothes need to be considered carefully to enable the pupil to have credibility with his/her peers. Consider how fashions can be adapted to make dressing easier.
- Adapt clothes with elastic, Velcro, e.g. cut the school tie and join with Velcro, adapt cuffs by putting in elastic to allow the hand to fit through.
- Use 'curly laces', wear polo shirts, jumpers with logos to help orientation, jumpers with raglan sleeves, belts with a magnetic buckle.
- Allow extra time for dressing after PE. Discuss with the pupil as to whether they need support with the organisation and practicalities of dressing.
- Provide a basket or equivalent to place clothes in to aid organisation.
- Pupils may prefer to change in a quieter area if support is required or if a busy area is too distracting.

Independent toileting

- Parents should be encouraged to dress their child in clothes that are easy to pull up and down.
- Prompt cards can help to develop independent routines.
- Wet wipes should be available for pupils who find it difficult to cleanse themselves.
- Older pupils may prefer to use the accessible toilet.

Personal appearance

- Pupils may be unaware of their appearance, making them vulnerable to teasing.
- Encourage pupils to check appearance in mirrors placed in toilets.

Eating

Pupils with co-ordination difficulties may find it difficult to develop good eating habits. Younger pupils often dislike foods with variable textures, find it difficult to manipulate cutlery, preferring to finger-feed, and may have poor oral skills which makes chewing more difficult. This may continue to cause difficulties as pupils get older.

Younger pupils

- Play with spoons to scoop sand, shaving foam, imitation peas.
- Practise using plastic knives and forks to cut playdough, clay, etc.

- Some pupils with co-ordination difficulties may not easily tolerate food at extremes of temperatures and may not like combinations of textures of food on a plate, e.g. meat, vegetables and gravy.
- Encourage parents to practise feeding at home:
    - carry out activities which use two hands together, e.g. peeling a banana;
    - practise spooning shaving foam, sand from one container to another;
    - give food which can be 'stabbed' with a fork;
    - use a knife to slice soft foods, e.g. banana, progressing to harder foods;
    - use a spoon and fork (of an appropriate size and shape) with soft foods.
- Use Dycem to stabilise dishes.
- Moulded cutlery helps place fingers in the correct place.
- Adapted cutlery with built-up handles can help pupils with weak wrists.

Developing coping strategies

Some pupils may always find it difficult to eat appropriately and may need encouragement to develop coping strategies:

- Select food which is easier to eat, e.g. mashed potato rather than spaghetti.
- Have a packed lunch rather than a cooked meal.
- Have a tissue/wet wipe in the lunch box or pocket, to wipe the face after eating.
- Have a small mirror in the lunch box or pocket to check that the face is clean.
- Acknowledge that the pupil may find a busy dining hall a difficult situation, i.e. negotiating the space between tables, carrying a tray, using cutlery, the close proximity of other pupils etc. Support by:
    - allowing the pupil to go earlier (with a friend);
    - supporting the carrying of a tray;
    - finding a quiet area to sit.

36 Dressing skills progression and checklist

Children acquire dressing skills in a hierarchical manner. Some children with co-ordination difficulties will take longer to develop these skills, but when teaching they should still be addressed in the order below.

Approximate age	Skill development
1 year	☐ co-operates in dressing, e.g. holds foot up for shoe to be put on ☐ puts hat on head ☐ takes off socks.
2 years	☐ has the prerequisite skills to lift arms above the head and maintain balance ☐ pulls off an unfastened coat, tries to put on socks, tries to pull down trousers ☐ tries to put on a coat ☐ finds armholes in a T-shirt ☐ unbuttons a large button.
3 years	☐ perceptually aware of more details, e.g. where armholes are ☐ improved balance when sitting while reaching above the head ☐ is able to reach behind the back ☐ pulls down trousers, skirts independently ☐ can put on socks and shoes ☐ can put on front-fastening garments ☐ requires help with T-shirts ☐ is able to fasten large buttons, pull up zips.
4 years	☐ behind the back co-ordination develops ☐ can remove a T-shirt, jumper ☐ can fasten buckles and fasten a separating zip ☐ is able to put on socks, shoes ☐ can distinguish between the front and back of clothes.
5 years	☐ is able to balance ☐ puts on a jumper, T-shirt correctly orientated ☐ can now dress unsupervised.

Approximate age	Skill development
6 years	☐ can tie laces ☐ can fasten buttons behind the back.
8 years	☐ has the ability to select the correct clothes for the weather.
10 years	☐ can tie a necktie.

Reference

Adapted from Dunn Klein, M. (1983) *Pre-Dressing Skills*, Winslow Press.

37 Teaching dressing skills

The child with co-ordination difficulties frequently struggles to take off and put on his/her coat and shoes, and change for PE. Dressing skills should be:

- taught in a hierarchical order (see Dressing skills progression, Chapter 36);
- taught using the backward chaining method, where the child completes the final small step of the task;
- carried out with the child in a stable position, e.g. by sitting on a chair, on the floor with the back resting against the wall;
- practised with oversized garments before using actual clothing.

Taking shoes off	*Putting shoes on*

1. The child takes hold of a single lace or the Velcro strap and loosens it;	1. The child holds the shoe open, pushes the tongue back;
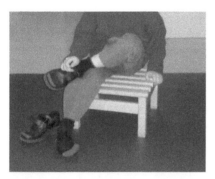	
2. pulls the tongue of the shoe forward then pushes the shoe off, using the other foot or by hand.	2. pushes the foot into the shoe (it might help to place the toe of the shoe against a hard surface).

Taking socks off	*Putting socks on*

1. The child tucks the thumbs into the top of the sock;	1. The child holds the sock open at the top and folds it over slightly;
	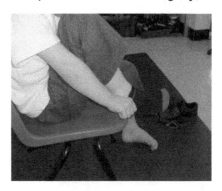
2. pushes the sock down past the heel;	2. hooks his/her thumbs in the top and places it over the big toe;

3. holds the toe end and pulls it off.	3. pulls it up over the heel.

Taking a jumper off (same method can be used for T-shirts and coats)

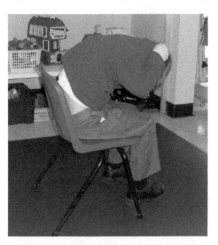

1. The child grasps the collar or neck at the back of the garment, pulls it over the head while keeping the head down;

2. pulls one arm out (weaker side first) then pulls out the other arm.

Putting a jumper on

1. The child lays the jumper out on the table or lap with the back uppermost and the opening nearest the tummy;

2. pushes one arm into the sleeve, making sure the hand comes right out of the cuff (weaker arm in first); repeats with other arm;

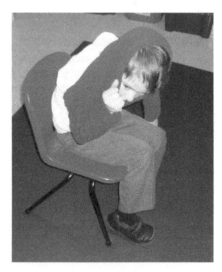

3. leans forward, tucks the chin down and pulls the jumper over the head.

Putting a coat on

1. The child lays the coat on the table or lap with the lining uppermost and the hood or collar next to the tummy;

2. pushes one arm into the sleeve, making sure the hand comes out of the cuff (weaker side first); repeats with the other arm;

3. stretches out the arms and lifts them over the head keeping the chin tucked down;

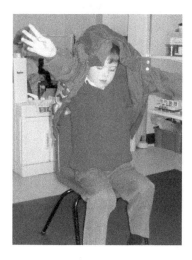

4. sits up straight and wriggles to make the coat fall into place on the back.

Taking trousers off (also shorts and pants)

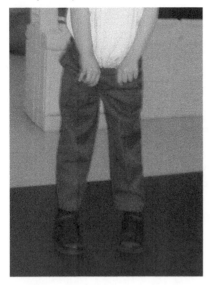

1. The child tucks thumbs into the waistband;

2. pushes the trousers down over the hips and knees, holding on with one hand;

3. or sits down and pushes the trousers down over the feet.

Putting trousers on (also shorts and pants)

1. The child sits on a chair;

2. or on the floor to put legs in;

3. rolls from side to side, pulling trousers up over the hips;

4. or sits on the chair then stands holding on with one hand as in picture 2 opposite centre.

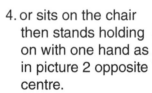

If the child's standing balance is insecure, encourage him/her to hold onto a static object or sit down.

38 Communication and social skills

Some pupils with co-ordination difficulties may have problems with communication skills. The following suggestions may support these pupils.

Foundation Stage

Difficulty	Strategies
Plays alone rather than in a group	• set up play situations for two children involving turn-taking, support the play with explicit words, Sam's turn, Amy's turn (build up the number of children in the group) • support the interaction of the pupil at playtime with adult led games, e.g. 'Ring-a-Ring o' Roses'.
Lack of imaginative play	• model play in the 'house' corner • support play in model-making areas.
Difficulty following simple routines and instructions	• use a visual timetable with simple photographs, to show the routine of the session (in an individual format or for the whole class) • give simple instructions, one at a time • support instructions with visual prompts, e.g. point to where the item should be placed when gluing; model activities • use 'hand-over-hand' movements to demonstrate what is expected • play games which encourage listening skills, e.g. simplified version of 'Simon Says ...'.
Unclear speech	• ask the family to check with the GP regarding possible hearing problems • possible speech and language therapy (SALT) assessment required • encourage participation in singing rhymes, copying rhythms with musical instruments • encourage use of non-verbal language: gestures, pictures, signs to accompany speech • give choices in a sentence which require a short response rather than a long one, e.g. 'Do you want to play with the garage or the bricks?', as this requires a short answer rather than an attempt at a whole sentence • praise and respond to attempts to communicate.

Difficulty	Strategies
Poor eye contact	• sit facing the pupil when working/playing together • hold objects which are being discussed up to the face, to encourage looking at the speaker.

Primary pupils

Difficulty	Strategies
Poor eye contact	• encourage by saying 'look at my face', avoid insisting on eye contact • sit opposite rather than alongside when working with the pupil.
Daydreams	• seat close to the teacher for whole-class input • place in a work area which is as distraction-free as possible (away from windows, displays) • give gentle prompts (written or spoken) to encourage a return to task.
Poor articulation, difficulty organising speech	• SALT input • reduce pressure on the pupil; it may be better to avoid questioning in large groups • give cues if word finding is a problem, e.g. give the initial sound of the word • use a home/school book for parents to say what has been done at home to help the pupil at news time and for school to show what has been achieved, in order for the pupil to talk about what has been done at school.
Slow to process information and give feedback, either verbal or physical	• give name first to ensure pupil knows he is being addressed • allow time to respond to questions, instructions • avoid unnecessary words in instructions • keep instructions short and to the point and give in the order in which the activity is to take place • ask the pupil to vocalise what he/she has to do • put instructions for work to be completed on the board • use cue cards as prompts to start/finish an activity • minimise background noise when giving instructions.
Develops avoidance strategies	• give positive feedback • support difficult activities • provide alternative recording strategies • see Promoting self-esteem (Chapter 39).
Asks excessive questions	• have a rule: only one answer will be given to a question • be prepared to repeat an instruction and give written/verbal support to the pupil when he/she is beginning a task • give praise when a task is being carried out in order to provide reassurance.

Secondary pupils

Difficulty	Strategies
Unable to follow complex instructions	• have instructions for the lesson on the board or printed out • ensure instructions for homework are understood; give a slip of paper with them on to take home.
Difficulty sequencing events, particularly in written format	• give picture cues or written prompts when writing up an experiment • encourage the use of storyboards for story writing.
Poor speech production	• avoid asking questions in a large group • refrain from asking the pupil to read aloud if he/she is uncomfortable with this.
Social isolation	• use buddy systems • give opportunities to learn about social skills: giving eye contact, listening to the other speakers, giving them time to talk • encourage and support group working • encourage the pupil to take part in school clubs • have designated areas, e.g. SEN areas which provide a quiet place for pupils who lack the social skills to cope at lunchtimes • have supervised activities, e.g. card games which help to develop social skills • use Social Stories (Carol Gray).
Pre-occupation with topics or subjects	• channel the pupil's pre-occupation with particular interests into topic work where possible • teach that it is only appropriate to talk about one's particular interests for a certain length of time • use pupil's interests to support others, e.g. teaching computer skills if that is the particular interest.

39　Promoting self-esteem

Pupils may have a poor self-image for a number of reasons:

- They may feel incompetent and frustrated because of difficulties in carrying out day-to-day tasks, resulting in inappropriate behaviour or becoming withdrawn.
- Pupils with co-ordination difficulties may have difficulty relating to their peers for a number of reasons:
    - having unco-ordinated movements which result in their bumping into others, knocking over their equipment, etc;
    - lacking gross motor skills, so that they do not get picked for teams at playtime and in PE lessons;
    - having a poor tactile system which results in rough play;
    - having inappropriate social skills;
    - being vulnerable to bullying;
    - being perceived by their peers as someone who cannot write neatly, draw well, cut neatly, eat their food appropriately, etc.
- Pupils may be perceived inappropriately, i.e. lazy, naughty.
- Adolescent growth spurts can make problems worse; pupils have to develop co-ordination over again.

Strategies to develop pupils' self-esteem

- The teacher should be a good role model to other pupils in the class, in respect to the pupil with co-ordination difficulties, by showing understanding of the pupil's difficulties rather than by being irritated by them.
- In the Foundation Stage:
    - give play opportunities to encourage appropriate interaction with peers, e.g. supporting imaginative play in the home corner, offering turn-taking games;
    - offer construction-type toys which are easier to manipulate, e.g. 'Clic' wooden pieces which connect with press studs, 'Stickle Bricks', 'magnetic block' shapes which connect easily with magnets. Encourage and support this type of play activity in order that the children can create models they are proud of.

- Provide activities which are at the appropriate level to avoid frustration.
- Identify areas of difficulty and use a small-steps approach to interventions.
- Allow pupils to compete against themselves rather than with their peers.
- Set up gross motor groups to improve motor co-ordination, which provide success (see page 141).

- Provide alternative recording strategies which allow the pupil to produce some attractive pieces of work (see page 92).
- Acknowledge that a much greater effort is required to complete a task than for some other pupils and praise accordingly, rather than making comments such as 'hurry up', 'work faster'.
- Mark work according to content rather than appearance.
- Use circle time to focus on strengths.
- Observe the pupil at breaktimes to ascertain if isolation is an issue. If so, set up buddy systems and, occasionally, alternatives to playtime, e.g. encourage pupils to work on a computer together. Introduce games supported by older pupils or dinner supervisors.
- Introduce games in the playground which are supported by a classroom assistant, lunchtime supervisor or older pupils.
- Encourage coping strategies, e.g. providing a packed lunch which is easily eaten, instead of a cooked lunch that may allow poor eating habits to be revealed.
- Support the pupil to develop organisational skills so that he/she does not disrupt or annoy other pupils, e.g. avoid them spreading into another pupil's working area by marking out a working area and encourage staying within it. Provide storage into which pupils can put belongings and encourage sorting it out regularly (this may need support).
- It may be possible to set up situations where a pupil is able to demonstrate strengths and teach another pupil, e.g. how to use a new game on the computer.
- Give the pupil responsibility e.g. carrying out jobs within the classroom.
- Use a buddy system to support appropriate movement around school.
- Be aware that some pupils may be easily led as they may take language literally and do as their peers tell them.
- Some pupils could be vulnerable to teasing and bullying, which would need to be addressed.

40   Personal organisation

Secondary transfer

Moving to a new school can be daunting for any pupil, especially those with coordination and organisational difficulties. The following suggestions are intended to help prepare pupils for a successful transition period.

Area of concern	Suggestions
Sharing information with the new school	<ul><li>primary schools will automatically share information with the receiving school</li><li>parents can arrange to meet with the SENCO at the new school before their child transfers to discuss individual needs or concerns</li><li>parents should put their points in writing to make sure everything is covered during the meeting.</li></ul>
Getting to know the new school	<ul><li>consider additional visits prior to transfer</li><li>provide a plan of the new school; give information about one-way systems in corridors and stairs; how lunchtime is organised</li><li>help the pupil familiarise him-/herself with the layout of the building</li><li>when timetables are distributed encourage the pupil to colour-code each subject and cross-reference this to colour-coded rooms on the school building plan</li><li>be aware that the pupil may find it difficult to adapt to the new situation and could be prone to outbursts, etc. Ensure the pupil is aware of the rules and expectations. A 'buddy' may help to support.</li></ul>
Personal organisition	<ul><li>prepare timetables using a computer, with colour coding: one colour for each lesson, with a colour matched to the equipment needed and the same colour for the homework from that lesson</li><li>encourage covering exercise and textbooks in a colour that corresponds with the timetable and school plan;</li><li>encourage the use of a set of clear plastic wallets to organise all the books and equipment needed for each subject (match to the colour system described above)</li></ul>

Area of concern	Suggestions
	• have a duplicate pencil, pen and ruler in each wallet as this will reduce the need for organising writing equipment at the beginning and end of each lesson • encourage and support the use of a locker rather than have the pupil carry everything around all day • the pupil may need support with organising possessions • support payment of lunch in the easiest manner within the school system (packed lunch may be the easiest as it requires the least organisation) • consider specific arrangements at lunch time, i.e. going first when it is quietest, support to carry trays, sitting closest to the serving hatch to avoid the difficulty of negotiating tables.
PE	• give extra instructions, one at a time; consider hand-over-hand methods to learn the use of equipment • don't ask the pupil to go first – allow him to watch and take cues regarding how to complete a task • give extra information about the rules and strategies of the game • consider small group work rather than full games • consider that low muscle tone will reduce stamina • extra time may be required for dressing in a quieter area • encourage using a mirror to ensure that clothes are replaced correctly.
Difficulty with written work/ copying from the board/organising work	• if ICT equipment is available and keyboard skills are weak, try to provide extra practice so that ICT options can be used for longer pieces of written work, both at home and at school • writing quality may deteriorate or writing may be very difficult to read; ask for PowerPoint notes, part-prepared handouts • avoid copying from the board and provide the above • extra time may be required for work to be finished (but not in break time) • try to monitor exercise books and watch out for comments about unfinished work; make an appointment to discuss any concerns with the SENCO • templates, lines to give guidance to where work should be placed.
Difficulty with drawing	• provide pre-drawn diagrams or stencils.

Area of concern	Suggestions
Managing homework	• try homework slips, homework written in the diary by an adult, teacher checking the homework diary to ensure it has been completed, use of a Dictaphone to record homework, homework being circulated by email, homework being posted on the school website.
Social issues	• offer access to a quieter area, e.g. in the SEN area • encourage the joining of lunchtime clubs • use 'Social Stories'.

41 Suggestions for teenagers

Revising for exams

Some suggestions which may help you to be successful:

- Revise with a friend, talk ideas through together.
- Break your notes up into sections, rather than trying to revise a large section at once.
- Use all your senses: listen to tapes (made by yourself or commercial ones), read notes, watch DVDs, write out what you have learned using highlighter pens to mark the main points.
- Have plenty of drinks of water and eat dried fruit, apricots, etc., while you are working.
- Find silly ways to remember things.
- Plan to give yourself a reward when you have done the revision you needed to do.
- Your school may be able to gain extra time and ICT equipment (if this is your usual method of recording work) for you to do your exams.
- Use apps such as 'Inspiration Maps' (www.inspiration.com) to structure and focus revision.

Sports activities outside school

When choosing a sports activity, consider:

- Team games require the co-ordination of a lot of movements, quick responses, and may also involve pressure from other team members and be more difficult to take part in.
- Activities such as aerobics, line dancing require a sequence of movements and a faster response, which can prove disheartening when it is difficult to keep up.
- Solitary sports such as weight building, golf, fishing and horse riding give more time to think and respond and may be more satisfying.
- Activities which allow for self-competition can boost self-esteem: gym activities, running, golf, swimming.
- Try badminton, tennis, table tennis, etc., with a non-competitive friend.
- Aqua aerobics, Pilates and yoga provide slower forms of exercise and promote relaxation.
- Some activities can help improve co-ordination: judo, karate, archery and snooker; swimming helps build up strength on both sides of the body.
- Games on a Wii provide an alternative form of exercise.
- Explore activities for youngsters with physical difficulties within the local area.

Hobbies

Developing a satisfying hobby can be a good form of relaxation, a way of socialising if carried out at a class or club, and a way to boost self-esteem. Enjoyable hobbies could include:

- listening to music, which can be relaxing;
- playing an instrument, which requires the correct choice of instrument to ensure that it is not a cause of frustration;
- working with clay, which makes less exacting demands than other craft activities;
- creative writing (using a word processor);
- photography, which can produce satisfying results;
- playing draughts or chess, which develops memory and planning.

Organising yourself at home/school

Some suggestions for making life easier:

- Use a large diary to write a list of things to be done; an electronic organiser could help.
- Use Post-it notes in the bedroom, etc., for reminders of things to take to school, reminders of jobs to be done.
- Have a list of things that may need to be taken to school: bus pass/money, lunch box/lunch money, etc., and pin it near the door; check the night before that you have put everything in your bag.
- Use transparent wallets with a coloured sticker for each subject; put equipment needed for each subject in the folder: matching pencil, exercise book with the same coloured dot.
- Have a rucksack with lots of pockets to store things in, rather than one big holdall where everything disappears at the bottom (tidy it out every day!).
- Have as little extra gear in your bedroom as possible.
- Have labelled boxes, trays to keep stuff in.
- Tidy up every day and have a chocolate bar for doing it!

Further reading

Addy, Lois (2004) *How to Understand and Support Children with Dyspraxia*, LDA

Addy, Lois and Dixon, Gill (2004) *Making Inclusion Work for Children with Dyspraxia: Practical Strategies for Teachers*, Routledge

Ball, Morven F. (2002) *Developmental Co-ordination Disorder: Hints and Tips for the Activities for Daily Living*, Jessica Kingsley

Biggs, Victoria (2005) *Caged in Chaos: A Dyspraxic Guide to Breaking Free* (written by a teenager with dyspraxia), Jessica Kingsley

Colley, Mary (2002) *Living with Dyspraxia: A Guide for Adults with Developmental Dyspraxia*, Dyspraxia Foundation

Dixon, Gill (2005) *Dyscover Yourself: A Book for Children with Dyspraxia* (a booklet for 7-, 8- and 9-year-olds to help them understand themselves), Dyspraxia Foundation

Dunn Klein, Marsha (1982) *Pre-Writing Skills: Skill Starters for Motor Development*, Communication Skill Builders

Dunn Klein, Marsha (1983) *Pre-Dressing Skills*, Winslow Press

Dunn Klein, Marsha (1987) *Pre-Scissor Skills*, Winslow Press

Henderson, Anne (2012) *Dyslexia, Dyscalculia and Mathematics: A Practical Guide*, Routledge

Latham, Clare and Ann Miles, Ann (1997) *Assessing Communication*, David Fulton Publishers

Macintyre, Christine (2000) *Dyspraxia in the Early Years*, David Fulton Publishers

Penso, Dorothy (1999) *Keyboarding Skills for Children with Disabilities*, Whurr Publishers

Portwood, Madelaine (1999) *Developmental Dyspraxia*, second edition, David Fulton Publishers

Ripley, Kate, Daines, Bob and Barrett, Jenny (1997) *Dyspraxia: A Guide for Teachers and Parents*, David Fulton Publishers

Sheridan, Mary (1999) *Spontaneous Play in Early Childhood: From Birth to Six Years*, Routledge

Practical ideas

Hill, Katy and Mark (2002) *Cutting Skills: Photocopiable Activities to Improve Scissor Technique*, LDA

Hill, Katy and Mark (2006) *Fine Motor Skills: Photocopiable Activities to Improve Motor Control*, LDA

Hill, Katy and Mark (2007) *Visual Perception Skills: Photocopiable Activities to Improve Visual Understanding*, LDA

Hill, Katy and Mark (2008) *Visual Memory Skills: Photocopiable Activities to Improve Visual Memory*, LDA

Hill, Katy and Mark (2012) *More Cutting Skills: Photocopiable Activities to Improve Scissor Technique*, LDA

ReLEASS (Regional LEA Support Services) (n.d.), *Ready Steady – Go to PE! Assessment and Activities for Early Gross Motor Skills: A Practical Guide for Teachers*, IPaSS, Francis Askew Centre, Hull

Sheridan, Mary (2014) *From Birth to Five Years: Children's Developmental Progress*, revised and updated by Ajay Sharma and Helen Cockerill, Routledge

Teodorescu, Ion and Addy, Lois (1998) *Write from the Start: Unique Programme to Develop the Fine Motor and Perceptual Skills Necessary for Effective Handwriting, 3 volumes*, LDA

Standards

Teachers Standards, 2012	Department of Education	www.abilitynet.org.uk
Special Educational Needs (SEN) Code of Practice 2014	Department of Education	www.gov.uk

Appendix 1   Management issues

These are whole-school issues to be considered by the senior management team when planning to meet the needs of a pupil with co-ordination difficulties.

Consideration	Yes	No	Action required
Are the governors aware of their responsibilities in ensuring that the needs of pupils with co-ordination difficulties are met?			
Is the quality of teaching for pupils with SEN and the progress made by pupils a core part of the school's performance management arrangements?			
Are all staff aware of the educational implications of co-ordination difficulties?			
Is there a need for additional adult support for the pupil?			
Are staff appropriately trained?			
Are effective communication arrangements between home and school in place?			
Are other agencies involved in meeting the needs of the pupil?			
Do you know where to seek further information and advice?			
Are you aware of recent legislation, i.e. government initiatives?			
Are there strategies to support the child's emotional well-being?			
Are there strategies to promote positive peer-group relationships?			
Do you promote positive images of the child?			
Are appropriate teaching strategies in place?			
Are any additional resources required to support curriculum delivery?			

Appendix 2   Pupil Profile checklists

Pupil Profile 1

Name: .... Class: .... Date: ....

Area of development	Observed difficulties (Foundation Stage)
Sensory	☐ very excitable, making shrill or loud noises, hand flapping ☐ cannot sit still during circle or story time ☐ limited concentration, flitting from one activity to another ☐ distressed by high levels of noise ☐ dislikes being touched or avoids certain textures ☐ fiddles, chews objects or clothes ☐ poor safety awareness or a fear of heights ☐ fussy eater.
Gross motor skills	☐ clumsy movements, bumps into objects, falls, trips ☐ easily knocked off-balance ☐ difficulty climbing on a small climbing frame ☐ difficulty getting into or onto play equipment and chairs ☐ jumps from inappropriate heights with no sense of danger ☐ has to squat to pick up toys from the floor ☐ difficulty getting up from the floor without using hands ☐ difficulty jumping with both feet together ☐ difficulty pedalling a tricycle ☐ climbs the stairs leading with one foot ☐ difficulty throwing, catching and kicking a large ball.
Fine motor skills	☐ uncertain of hand dominance ☐ avoids jigsaws and construction toys ☐ poor pencil grip ☐ unable to use scissors ☐ struggles to build tower of 6 one-inch cubes.
Independence skills	☐ difficulty taking off coat and hanging it on a peg ☐ struggles with undressing ☐ unable to use the toilet independently ☐ messy eater, prefers to finger-feed ☐ spills drinks.
Communication	☐ plays alone rather than in a group ☐ lack of imaginative play ☐ difficulty following simple routines and instructions ☐ unclear speech, cannot speak in sentences ☐ avoidance of eye contact.

Pupil Profile 2

Name: .... Class: .... Date: ....

Area of development	Observed difficulties (Key Stages 1 and 2)
Sensory	☐ easily distracted, lacks persistence ☐ unable to use space effectively in PE or playground ☐ difficulty judging distance and direction ☐ difficulty sitting still ☐ dislikes being touched ☐ can be rough in play without realising ☐ irrational fear of open space or heights ☐ poor self-image, attention-seeking behaviour or withdrawn, underactive, reluctant to participate ☐ lacks inhibition ☐ poor visual tracking ☐ difficulty copying from the board ☐ dribbles from mouth.
Gross motor skills	☐ awkward, clumsy, bumps into people and objects ☐ poor balance ☐ difficulty with hopping, jumping, skipping ☐ poor ball skills ☐ difficulty learning new tasks or sequences.
Fine motor skills	☐ poor sitting posture ☐ uncertain of hand dominance ☐ immature pencil grasp and poor pencil control ☐ poor drawing skills, messy when using paints ☐ difficulty with using scissors ☐ avoids handwriting tasks ☐ finds it hard to set out work in books ☐ unable to construct a model following a diagram or plan.
Independence skills	☐ slow, messy eater, difficulty using cutlery ☐ slow to change for PE, mixes up order and orientation of clothes ☐ finds it hard to organise belongings ☐ avoids using the toilet at school.
Communication	☐ poor eye contact ☐ daydreams ☐ poor articulation, difficulties organising speech ☐ slow to process information and give feedback (verbal or physical) ☐ develops avoidance strategies ☐ asks excessive questions.
Organisation	☐ unable to remember messages ☐ forgets, cannot find dinner money ☐ cannot cope with changes of routine ☐ difficulties selecting equipment for a lesson or activity:

131

Pupil Profile 3

Name: .... Class: .... Date: ....

Area of development	Observed difficulties (Key Stages 3 and 4)
Sensory	☐ low self-esteem ☐ little sense of personal safety ☐ poor road sense as a pedestrian or cyclist ☐ difficulty coping with board work in class.
Gross motor skills	☐ difficulties in PE and games activities ☐ reluctant to participate in team games ☐ evidence of motor stereotypes such as hand-flapping.
Fine motor skills	☐ difficulty keeping up with written work ☐ books untidy with work being difficult to read and mark ☐ short written responses which do not match verbal ability ☐ unable to manipulate ruler, compass, protractor ☐ struggles in practical subjects.
Independence skills	☐ avoids removing jumper/sweatshirt in very hot weather ☐ lack of attention to personal appearance ☐ avoids eating with cutlery ☐ personal hygiene lacks attention.
Communication	☐ unable to follow complex instructions ☐ difficulty sequencing events, particularly in written format ☐ poor speech production ☐ socially isolated ☐ preoccupied with topics or subjects.
Organisation	☐ carries all belongings for fear of forgetting something ☐ loses books and writing equipment ☐ encroaches into his/her neighbour's personal space.

Appendix 3   Progression of drawing skills

Pupils learn to copy the following shapes in sequential order:

Group 1

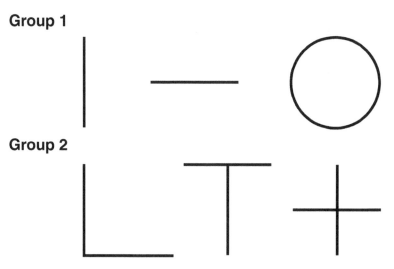

Group 2

The teaching of handwriting may begin once groups 1 and 2 have been mastered.

Group 3

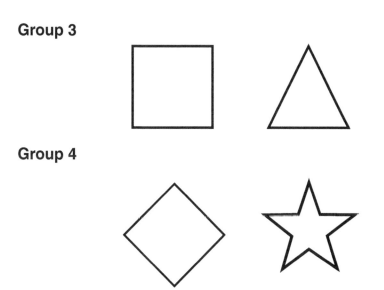

Group 4

NB: Pupils cannot copy a shape in a later group unless they can copy a shape from an earlier group.

Shape copying test

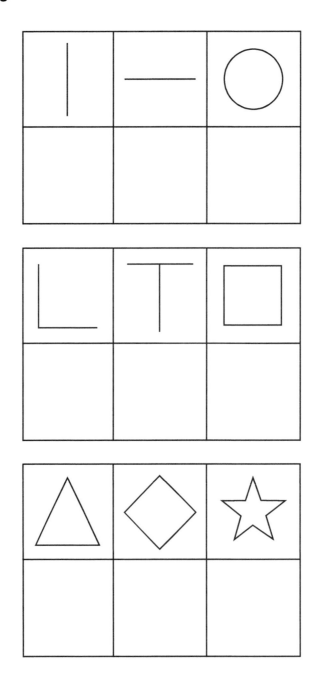

Appendix 4   Handwriting assessment form

Handwriting samples

Name: .... DOB: ....

Tick the appropriate box:

Comments:

1. Sits correctly — Yes ☐   No ☐
2. Handedness — Right ☐   Left ☐
3. Angles paper — Yes ☐   No ☐
4. Fixes with free hand — Yes ☐   No ☐
5. Problems with grasp — Tripod ☐   Immature tripod ☐
   Other ☐ ....
6. Pressure — Too much ☐   Too little ☐
7. Incorrect formation — ....
   (e.g. clockwise 'o's) ....
   ....
8. Reversals of letters — Left/Right   Top/Bottom
9. Erratic sizing — Yes ☐   No ☐
10. Poor alignment — Yes ☐   No ☐
11. Lack of spacing — Yes ☐   No ☐
12. Writing laborious — Yes ☐   No ☐
13. Fluency/speed — Slow ☐   Fast ☐
14. Mixed upper- and — Yes ☐   No ☐
    lower-case
15. Size of writing — Large ☐   Small ☐   Age-appropriate ☐

Poor grasp produces problems in areas 6, 12 and 13. See page 67 if there is a concern.

Strategies to be trialled:

Change in grasp: .... Other: (e.g. 'Write from the Start')
Pen/pencil grip: ....
Pen/pencil: ....
Angled board: ....
Date assessed: .... Reassessment date:.........................

Sample 1

Name: ....

```
┌─────────────────────────────────────────────────────────┐
│                                                           │
│                                                           │
│                                                           │
│                                                           │
│                                                           │
│                                                           │
│                                                           │
│                                                           │
│                                                           │
│                                                           │
│                                                           │
│                                                           │
│                                                           │
│                                                           │
│                                                           │
│                                                           │
│  **Place drawing here**                                   │
│                                                           │
└─────────────────────────────────────────────────────────┘
```

_____

_____

_____

_____

Date assessed: .... Reassement date: ....

Sample 2

Copy the following:

a b c d e f g h i j k l m n o p q r

s t u v w x y z

Check letter formation by copying the following sentence:

The cat sat on the mat.

Place drawing here

Date assessed:................................. Reassessment date: ....

Sample 3

Name: .... Date: ....

Handwriting speed – the Wold sentence copy test

> **Four men and a jolly boy came out of the black and pink house quickly to see the bright violet sun but the sun was behind a cloud.**
>
> _____
>
> _____
>
> _____
>
> _____
>
> Speed in letters per minute: ....

Instructions

Ask the pupil to copy the sentence onto the lines above using his/her neatest handwriting. Divide the time taken (remembering to convert seconds into a percentage of a minute) by the number of characters (103). This will give the speed in letters per minute.

Minutes and seconds	%
5 secs	.08
10 secs	.17
15 secs	.25
20 secs	.33
25 secs	.42
30 secs	.50
35 secs	.58
40 secs	.67
45 secs	.75
50 secs	.83
55 secs	.92

Age	Letters per minute
7	20–25
8	30
9	40
10	50
11	60
12	67
13	75
14	80

Sample 4

Pupil: .... Date: ....

Handwriting speed – the Wallen, Bonney and Lennox test

---

the quick brown fox jumps over the lazy dog.

_____

_____

_____

_____

_____

_____

_____

_____

_____

Speed in letters per minute: ....

Instructions

Ask the pupil to copy the sentence as many times as possible in three minutes. Count the number of letters written and divide this total by the number of minutes. Use the table below to determine speed in letters per minute.

Age	Letters per minute
7	54
8	57
9	67
10	81
11	94

Age	Letters per minute
12	100
13	115
14	116
15	124
16	133

© 2015, *Supporting Children with Dyspraxia and Motor Co-ordination Difficulties*
Coulter, Kynman, Morling, Grayson and Wing, Routledge

Appendix 5   Number template sample

The arrow indicates the direction in which the number operation is completed.

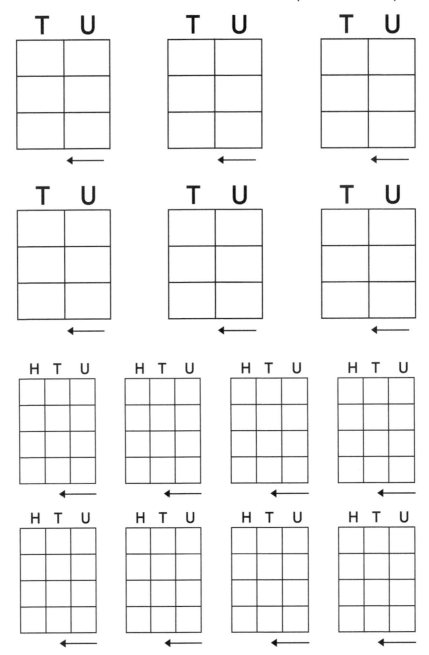

Appendix 6 Parental handout 1

Improving your child's motor co-ordination skills

You can help your child improve their co-ordination skills in a number of ways. However, anything which is done should be fun and not add pressure to you or your child.

Younger children

Gross motor skills

- make family visits to play areas which incorporate ball pools, tunnels, climbing equipment; visit parks with climbing frames, slides over safe flooring;
- walk to school;
- encourage running, jumping, hopping, skipping;
- make obstacle courses through furniture/in the garden, for the child to crawl through;
- play balloon, ball games (choose a ball of the right size and weight that your child can catch);
- play darts with a Velcro board;
- play at catching a ball with the child using a Velcro catcher;
- skittle games;
- make targets: how many times can you throw a beanbag into a waste bin, improving the targets on a weekly basis; progress by moving the bin further away or by making a smaller target.

Fine motor skills

- activities to improve hand skills:
    - rolling pastry;
    - playing with playdough;
    - squeezing sponges at bath time;
    - popping bubble wrap;
    - pegging out dolls clothes;
    - finger puppets, finger rhymes;
    - pick-a-stick games;
- provide a variety of pens with different barrels, chalks, large pieces of paper such as lining paper;
- play with toys such as 'Etch a Sketch';

- play drawing games: the parent draws a face shape and encourages the child to put on features (use a mirror to look at features). The same approach can be made when drawing a house or car (pictures may help).

Body awareness

- ask your child to put bubbles on different parts of the body when playing in the bath;
- naming body parts in pictures in books;
- playing games, e.g. 'Simon Says ...', 'Hokey Cokey';
- playing games in front of a long mirror.

Auditory discrimination

- read familiar stories and pause for your child to fill in the missing word or read it incorrectly so that you can be corrected;
- tell a joke (of an appropriate length) and ask them to repeat it to another family member; play listening games, e.g. 'Grandma Went to Market and Bought ...'.

Sensory sensitivity

- improve tactile skills (touch) by introducing finger paints, reading books which have pages with different textures within the story, rolling/crawling on different surfaces, e.g. carpet, hard floor;
- guessing what the toy is in a feely bag before it's pulled out.

Visual perception

- play matching games: dominoes, snap, pairs;
- jigsaws (with adult help).

Older children

Gross motor skills

- play 'wheelbarrow' games;
- play push/pull games, tug of war;
- encourage individual sports activities, e.g. body building, golf, judo, swimming rather than team games;
- play swingball;
- practise the skills required in PE lessons in a number of ways: make 'hockey sticks' with rolled-up cardboard and play with a foam ball; play tennis with short-handled plastic racquets and soft balls;
- play on the Wii.

Fine motor skills

- offer a variety of pens with different grips (available from stationers) to see which are easiest and most comfortable to use;
- select images from the internet to provide alternatives to drawings when illustrating work;
- use templates from art shops to help with science work;
- help the child follow instruction to make models with Lego;
- use 'apps' on ICT equipment to develop letter formation;
- encourage the development of typing skills.

Visual perception

- 'dot to dot' books;
- word searches;
- 'Where's Wally?' books, 'Where's the Meerkat?' books;
- play bowls;
- remote control cars.

Remember to praise your child and be patient (and encourage this with the child's peers, too).

Appendix 6 Parental handout 2

Helping your child develop organisational skills

Help your child to become as independent as possible by trying the following ideas:

- Encourage the tidying up of toys with the use of transparent plastic boxes with picture labels.
- Encourage the organisation of equipment needed the next day, before going to bed.
- Use lists for daily checks when packing up personal necessities: dinner money/ pack up box, bus passes, etc. (see right); cross through when the item is packed.
- Whiteboards could be used to indicate what happens on each day and the equipment required: Monday is PE day so I need ....
- Use clear boxes with labels which help organisation as your child gets older, e.g. for fishing gear, toiletries.
- Buy a rucksack with pockets, elasticised places to help organisation, rather than a large holdall in which everything becomes a muddle.
- Use transparent pencil cases, wallets for reading books, equipment for particular subjects, e.g. protractor, compass, ruler, maths book.
- Ask teachers to check that homework diaries are completed correctly or check emails from school.
- Negotiate the time that should be spent on homework.
- Consider the use of a planner to organise when homework/ projects should be done so that completion dates can be met.
- Provide a quiet area to do homework with pens/laptop, rubber, ruler to hand;
- Support the printing out of work or the transfer of ICT work to a memory stick or equivalent.

Every day
~~Dinner money~~
~~Bus pass~~
Pencil case
PE kit
Planner
Monday
PE kit
Tuesday
Swimming gear
Wednesday
Cookery

Appendix 6   Parental handout 3

Helping your child develop dressing and personal care skills

There are a number of strategies which can be tried to make your child's life easier at school and to encourage his/her independence.

Clothing items that need to be taken to school

- Choose clothing for your child which will make dressing a little easier and allow more independence: shoes with Velcro fastenings, trousers/skirts with elasticated waistbands, clothes which are not tight, e.g. jogging bottoms rather than jeans (this will help with changing from PE and adjusting clothes after visiting the toilet).
- Attach a large split ring or key fob to the loop of a coat zip to make it easier to pull up.
- Replace the hanging tab inside the coat with a longer tab made with elastic, which will make it easier to place on a peg.
- Name all your child's belongings with name tabs or indelible ink.
- Have all belongings, e.g. bags, hats, in a particular colour or with the same logo to make them easier to find in the cloakroom.

Teaching dressing skills

Younger children

Decide what item of clothing you want to teach your child to take off first, then put on (this is the easiest order). Teach one item at a time. The following are ways of developing dressing skills:

- Backward chaining would be a useful method to teach putting on items of clothing, e.g. putting on trousers (use jogging bottoms):
  - help your child to put trousers on, as far as the knees; the child pulls trousers up independently;
  - help him/her put trousers on as far as the ankles; the child pulls up trousers independently;
  - put one leg in; the child continues;
  - the child is shown how to lay trousers out and put them on;
  - the child sits and independently puts trousers on.

- Encourage your child to sit on the floor with something behind, e.g. wall, settee, when dressing.
- Practise doing fasteners on 'dressing' dolls with large buttons, zips and Velcro, doing fastenings on Mum's and Dad's clothes.
- Practise with clothes which are much too large first; play dressing-up games with large clothes.
- Practise dressing at weekends or when there is more time.
- Use T-shirts/sweatshirts with a logo/design on the front to help with the orientation of clothes.
- Praise your child when he/she is trying to dress independently. Be patient!

Older children

- Mark shoes with a code to show which is right or left, e.g. stick half a smile shape or half a football shape in each shoe, which your child has to match together in order to put his/her shoes on the right feet.
- Place your child's clothes on the bed in the order they are to be put on to help him/her dress more independently.
- Use a cue card to encourage dressing without help.

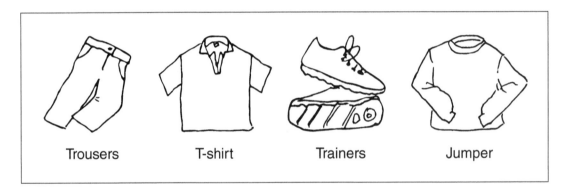

| Trousers | T-shirt | Trainers | Jumper |

- Time how many minutes it takes to dress and make a competition to see if your child can improve the time (taking care not to cause anxiety).
- Clothes need to be considered carefully to enable the child to have credibility with his/her peers.
- Consider how fashions can be adapted to make dressing easier:
    - Adapt clothes, e.g. cut the school tie and join with Velcro or elastic; adapt cuffs by putting in elastic to allow the hand to fit through; put Velcro behind a button.
    - Wear polo shirts, jumpers with logos to help orientation, jumpers with raglan sleeves; wear a belt with a magnetic buckle.
    - Use 'elastic shoelaces' which allow shoes to be laced at home and slipped on and off at school. 'Coiler' shoelaces are elastic laces which do not require tying. The shoe is laced and the lace coils to keep it in place (available from Homecraft). A long shoehorn can also help with putting on shoes.

Personal care

Toileting

- Dress your child in clothes that are easy to pull up and down.
- Make sure he/she can sit safely on the toilet with feet on a step if necessary.
- Use wet wipes for cleansing after using the toilet.
- Consider the use of cue cards for children who find it difficult to establish a toileting routine.

| Check that you are clean | Wash your hands | Check in the mirror |

Personal appearance

- Encourage younger children to use a long mirror to help develop awareness of body size and shape.
- Encourage checking in a mirror before leaving the house; put a written checklist near the mirror, e.g.:

> ✓ **shirt tucked in**
> ✓ **hair combed**
> ✓ **zip fastened**
> ✓ **underwear not showing**
> ✓ **collar tucked in**

Developing eating skills

Younger pupils often dislike foods with variable textures, find it difficult to manipulate cutlery (preferring to finger-feed), and may have poor oral skills which make chewing more difficult.

- Practise using spoons, knives and forks in play situations, e.g. by spooning sand, cutting playdough, clay, etc.
- Practise feeding at home:

  - spoon yogurt;
  - give food which can be stabbed with a fork;
  - use a knife to slice soft foods, e.g. banana, progressing to harder foods;
  - use a spoon and fork with soft foods;
  - use a knife and fork.

- Some children with co-ordination difficulties may not tolerate different textures of food easily; introduce new textures gradually.
- Some children may prefer food at particular temperatures; introduce new temperatures of food gradually.
- Some children may not like a variety of foods on one plate; allow for this and gradually try to extend the types of food on the plate.
- Use Dycem or a damp tea towel to stabilise dishes.
- Moulded cutlery helps place fingers in the correct place.
- Adapted cutlery with built-up handles can help pupils with weak wrists.
- Give a packed lunch, which can be eaten with fingers.
- If a school lunch is preferred, check the menu and encourage your child to choose foods which are easy to eat.

Appendix 7   Visual timetable samples

KS1

Monday	Tuesday	Wednesday	Thursday	Friday
Literacy	Literacy	Literacy	Literacy	Literacy
Break	Break	Break	Break	Break
Numeracy	Numeracy	Numeracy	Numeracy	Numeracy
Lunch	Lunch	Lunch	Lunch	Lunch
History	Art	PE	ICT	RE
Music	ICT	Geography	Science	Story

KS2

Monday	Tuesday	Wednesday	Thursday	Friday
Literacy	$63 + \square = 100$ $32 \times 32 = 1024$ $\triangle \, \circ \, \square$ Maths	History	$63 + \square = 100$ $32 \times 32 = 1024$ $\triangle \, \circ \, \square$ Maths	PE
$63 + \square = 100$ $32 \times 32 = 1024$ $\triangle \, \circ \, \square$ Maths	RE	$63 + \square = 100$ $32 \times 32 = 1024$ $\triangle \, \circ \, \square$ Maths	Literacy	$63 + \square = 100$ $32 \times 32 = 1024$ $\triangle \, \circ \, \square$ Maths
Break	Break	Break	Break	Break
Literacy	Geography	Literacy	Music	Literacy
ICT	French	Science	PE	Art
Lunch	Lunch	Lunch	Lunch	Lunch
Geography	Science	ICT	Geography	French
D&T	History	Art	History	Science

Appendix 8   Useful contacts

Ability Net
(suggestions for the use of ICT)

www.abilitynet.org.uk

British Dyslexia Association
Tel: 0845 251 9003

www.bdadyslexia.org.uk

Contact a Family (CAF)

www.cafamily.org.uk

Down's Syndrome Association

www.downs-syndrome.org.uk

Dyspraxia Foundation

www.dyspraxiafoundation.org.uk

Handwriting Interest Group

www.handwritinginterestgroup.org.uk

Hypermobility Syndrome Association

www.hypermobility.org

The National Autistic Society

www.autism.org.uk

Appendix 9   Resources and suppliers

Resources to support fine motor development

Category	Item	Supplier
	Fine motor skills box	tts-group.co.uk
Scissors	Mounted table-top scissors	Peta (UK) Ltd, tts-group.co.uk
	Push-down table-top scissors	As above
	Dual control training scissors (L & R)	As above
	Mini 'easy grip' (loop) scissors	As above
	Long loop scissors (L & R)	As above
	Self-opening scissors	As above
	Self-opening long loop scissors	As above
	Comprehensive Assessment Kit	As above
	Fiskars Squeezers	NES Arnold
	Fiskars Junior scissors (L & R)	As above
	Fiskars scissors for kids	As above
	Self-opening scissors (L & R)	Smith & Nephew, Homecraft
Cutting skills	*Cutting Skills* (see Further reading)	LDA
	Developing Scissor Skills (see Further reading)	Peta (UK) Ltd
Pencil grips	Tri-go	Taskmaster Ltd
	Stubbi (same as Stetro)	As above
	Ultra grip	As above
	Comfort grip	As above
	Crossguard	As above
	Claw grip	As above
	Handiwriter (puts pencil into web of hand)	tts-group.co.uk
Dycem	Non-slip material on roll	Patterson Medical
	Self-adhesive strips (to make non-slip rulers)	As above

Category	Item	Supplier
Sloping writing surface	Write Angle	Complete Care Shop 0845 5194 734
	Write Start Desk	LDA
	Posture Pack	Back in Action 020 7930 8309
Pencils	Write Start pencils	Variety of online sources
	Berol Hand Hugger pencils	As above
	Noris Triplus Triangular pencils	As above
	S Move pens and pencils (L & R)	stabilo.com or many stationers
Pens	Berol Hand Hugger fibre tip pen	As above
	Rubber-barrelled pens of varying flows/ resistance	Most stationery shops
Practice paper	Tram-line handwriting paper (10 mm/6 mm)	Hope Education
Handwriting programmes	*Write from the Start*, 1 and 2 (see Further reading)	Available from internet sources
Compass	Safety compass	Hope Education
Rulers	Alligator Easy Grip ruler	NES Arnold, Taskmaster
	Make your own non-slip ruler by attaching 2 × 1 cm strips of self-adhesive Dycem to the back of the ruler	
Reading aids	Reading Helper	Reading Helper 0113 257 7796
	Reading Window/ruler	LDA, tts-group.co.uk
	Coloured overlays	tts-group.co.uk
Magnifying glass	Visualiser	primaryict.co.uk 01227 769400
Construction toys	Stickle Bricks	Yorkshire Purchasing Organisation
	Magnetic blocks	As above
	Clic blocks	As above
ICT programs	Clicker software	Crick Software

Resources to support PE

Beanbags	Available as rabbits, frogs and turtles	NES Arnold
	Sensory ball pack	Yorkshire Purchasing
Balls	Spordas spider ball	NES Arnold
	Koosh ball	As above
	Tail ball	As above
	Floater ball (large, light, slow-moving)	As above
	Plus balls (inflatable paper balls – very slow)	As above
	Easy Katch ball (tendrils)	Hope Education
	Rubber Flex Graball	As above
	Bump ball (easy catch)	tts-group.co.uk
	Sure Grip netball	tts-group.co.uk
	Play Catch net and ball	Cost Cutters Educational Supplies
Group work equipment	Balance sets	Hope Education
	Agility ladder	tts-group.co.uk
	Tactile discs (stepping game)	tts-group.co.uk
Basketball	Adjustable height basketball net	As above
	Little Sure Shot	Hope Education

Resources to support food technology

Non-slip mats	Dycem mats available individually or on a roll	ROMPA 08452301177
Holding equipment	Clyde grater, scraper and spike –integral grater and vegetable holder on a non-slip base	Complete Care Shop 0845 194 734
	Food preparation system – for those who have difficulty gripping	As above
	Pan handle holder – to prevent the pan moving while stirring with one hand	As above
	Kettle tilt – to assist with pouring	As above
Alternative cutting equipment	Rapid chopper – a single-hand-operated chopper with an integral blade	As above

Resources to support recording skills

Spelling	*An Eye for Spelling*, Charles Cripps	LDA
	Starspell (computer program)	Inclusive Technology
	Toe by Toe, Keda and Harry Cowling	www.toe-by-toe.co.uk
Number	Numbershark (computer program)	Inclusive Technology
Recording	WriteOnline (talking word processing)	Crick Software
	Co:Writer (word prediction)	Don Johnston
Planning	Kidspiration (notes, mind maps)	SEMERC
	Inspiration (similar but for older pupils)	As above
	Draft:Builder (as above)	Don Johnston

ICT equipment

Keyboard letter stickers	Lower-case stickers for younger pupils	Inclusive Technology
Big keys	Large keys (upper or lower case)	Inclusive Technology, SEMERC
Alternative mice	Roller balls, etc.	Inclusive Technology

Resources to support social skills

Home/school	Socially Speaking (book/game)	LDA
'Social Stories'	*The New Social Story Book*, Carol Gray	Future Horizons

Suppliers

Address	*Tel. no./web*	*Equipment*
Crick Software Ltd Crick House Boarden Close Moulton Park Northampton NN3 6LF	01604 671691 www.cricksoft.com/uk	Recording work
Hope Education (incorporating NES Arnold and Philip & Tacey) Hyde Buildings Ashton Road Hyde SK14 4SH	0845 120 2224 www.hope-education.co.uk	Fine motor and PE equipment, adapted furniture, writing slopes

Address	Tel. no./web	Equipment
Inclusive Technology Ltd Unit 8 Riverside Court Huddersfield Road, Delph Oldham OL3 5FZ	01457 819790 www.inclusive.co.uk	ICT equipment and software, iPad apps
LDA	01945 463441 www.ldalearning.com	Fine motor equipment
Nottingham Rehab Supplies	www.nrs-uk.co.uk	Adapted furniture, fine motor/PE/food technology equipment
Peta	01666 843 200 www.peta-uk.com	Scissors
SEMERC Angel House, Sherston Malmesbury SN16 OLH	www.semerc.com	ICT equipment and software
Taskmaster Ltd	0116 270 4286 www.taskmasteronline.co.uk	Pencil grips, scissors, fine motor equipment
Toe by Toe	www.toe-by-toe.co.uk	Reading manual
Yorkshire Purchasing	01924 824477 www.ypo.co.uk	Fine motor/PE equipment